Changed
by chance

Changed
by chance

My Journey of
triumph
over
tragedy

Elizabeth Barker

SHE WRITES PRESS

Published 2015
Printed in the United States of America
ISBN: 978-1-63152-810-1
Library of Congress Control Number: 2015939798

For information, address:
She Writes Press
1563 Solano Ave #546
Berkeley, CA 94707

She Writes Press is a division of SparkPoint Studio, LLC.

Names and identifying characteristics have been changed to protect the privacy of certain individuals.

This book is lovingly dedicated to
Lauren Elizabeth Barker
"The Little Imp"
4/16/86–4/29/89

Although your time with us was short, your memory and your love will last forever.
You taught us a lifetime of lessons and have gifted us with unforgettable, bittersweet memories. Your courage and your perpetual smile are daily inspirations.

You are my muse for this incredible book journey.

"Death leaves a heartache no one can heal,
Love leaves a memory no one can steal"

CONTENTS

Introduction

I t took me twenty years to write this book.
Not literally, of course. Once I finally began writing, it only took a few months to pen the story. It has, after all, been permanently etched in my memory since it all transpired. But it has taken me more than two decades to finally understand why I needed to share it with the world.

My saga began with the birth of my first child, my daughter, Lauren. What should have been a joyous occasion quickly soured when we received the shocking news that our precious baby had Down syndrome and was fighting for her life due to a serious heart defect. I'm hardly the only parent to have endured this kind of anguish, of course—but that was just the beginning. From the moment of Lauren's birth, our carefully planned lives and dreams began to unravel and fade away. What then began was a five-year roller-coaster ride of highs and lows and dangerous detours in my life.

This time period was fraught with medical mishaps, life-altering encounters, and a plethora of hardships. During those years of cruel surprises, wrenching change, and constant stress, my husband and I faced a litany of challenges. Uncaring or incompetent medical professionals. Greedy, unscrupulous insurance companies. Financial worries. My own serious health problems, brought on by an immune system ravaged by twenty-four/seven stress. Suffocating fear and anxiety. As one disaster inexplicably led to the next, I found myself asking unanswerable questions:

How and when is this all going to end?

Will we survive; do we even have a future?

And, most common of all, *WHY is this happening to us? What in the world did I do that could bring so much pain and suffering upon my family?*

This is not the place for specifics—dramatic encounters, medical conditions, procedures, diagnoses, and the rest. I'll get to all that later. What matters is that I survived and thrived. And in the process, I changed dramatically from the person I was when it all started. Before Lauren's birth, I was an earnest young woman with a rather naïve, trusting view of the world. I relied on the advice of authority figures and professionals, and I assumed my life would flow precisely along the course I had carefully planned. I suppose that we all do this. But as my family's misfortunes mounted, I found myself being pulled down into a spiral of defeat and facing frightening life-or-death scenarios. I realized that I had to change if I wanted to survive. And I did.

As time went on, I began to trust my instincts and my strong intuition. I discovered an inner strength that I had no idea existed. I found that I should and could do battle with medical providers, misguided caregivers, insurance bureaucracy, and disease . . . and win. The old Liz would have been beaten down by five years of challenges; the new Liz became a peaceful warrior. When Lauren's and my own illnesses hurled us back into the intimidations of the health-care system again, I refused to play nice. I asked hard questions. I did not accept subpar care. I sought lawyers and advocates for advice. I fought. And that resilience kept me going when part of me wanted to hide, sob, and scream in despair.

In short, I became a champion. I didn't ask to. Nobody wants to become indestructible because of circumstance. But I chose to adapt, and it changed my life. I recognized and accepted each challenge, I researched my choices, and then I reacted accordingly. My new game plan became "survival of the fittest." And that's one of the reasons why I've written this book—to share my lessons with you.

My story isn't all darkness and pain, of course. No story is. There were many bright and happy times along the way. This book is rich with anecdotes of family, friendships, and deep connections, old and new. It's also filled with contrasting points of view. Although I went through many harsh experiences—the cruelty of a nurse, the carelessness of a physician, the greed of a money-hungry HMO system that broke my heart—I was fortunate to encounter incredible kindness and compassion in the course of my journey. In particular, Lauren's birth ushered me into a world that I had never glimpsed before—a world in which I found some of the most caring and committed people I've ever been privileged to know. I'm friends with many of them to this day, and they continue to give me strength and hope.

From family members and friends to one insightful doctor who made it possible for me to give birth to my younger son, time after time the good outweighed the bad. Viewing my glass in this way, as half full rather than half empty, kept me sane and kept me going, as did the several "angel moments"—instances when a stranger came out of nowhere to rescue me—that touched my life. One angel pulled some strings and got an important procedure scheduled when all my efforts to do so had failed; another cajoled me into getting a screening that saved my life. I learned to heed these small miracles, these angel moments, as if God or the universe or life were whispering to me, "I know this is awful, but I haven't forgotten you, and you can get through this." And I did.

Still, all of these hardships, agonies, and angelic interventions wouldn't have convinced me to write a book if not for my interest in the spiritual and intuitive. To write a book like this, one needs a *purpose*. I found mine with an introduction to a mystic/astrologer friend midway through my period of hell. Over the years, during my annual readings, this man—a renowned healer and seer—told me that there was a reason for all of my past suffering. I was destined, he said, to become a speaker, an advocate, and a writer—to educate and inspire people on surviving tragedy and finding their inner champion.

I was astonished by his prediction; I hadn't considered myself any of those things! But as the years rolled on and I thought more about his prophecies, I began to understand that this was my destiny. Just as fate had altered my past and created hardships, it would also lead me to my future. And once again, I would need to rise to its challenges.

Then, two years ago, out of the blue, another miracle happened. I had an epiphany. That aha moment occurred right after I staged a successful event to honor Lauren and to fund raise for a charity that helps special needs children. It was that act, and the tremendous outpouring of support that I received for it, that made me realize what my life's mission should be going forward and that the mentors and angels who had come into my life over the past years were there to help me on this new journey—to guide me in learning the meaning of and lessons from those horrific years, and to use this knowledge to help others. This book, then, is the fulfillment of both a prophecy and a dream.

This book is also about strength and survival, and the importance of the mind, body, and spirit connection—of keeping them all in sync. In my sadness over Lauren's illnesses, I became afflicted with my own. Some were the result of medical malpractice; others initially seemed like yet another bad roll of the dice. But I have come to realize that the monstrous stress I experienced during those years crippled my spirit as well as my immune system, leaving me vulnerable to deadly disease.

In this book, I'll talk about my revived understanding that true health is a matter of caring for body, mind, and spirit as a single unit—of respecting our own natural healing powers and the role of will and toughness in both preventing disease and bouncing back from it. The same mystic who predicted that I would become a speaker and champion also made a prediction about my health that

I wish I'd heeded but didn't. I learned the hard way that we're not machines. We're spiritual beings experiencing a physical existence. And it's only when we acknowledge our true nature that we become capable of true healing.

Tragedy and disease tried to take not just my family and my career but also my health and my life. I fought back, however, and I won. I'm living proof that no battle is hopeless.

Sometimes when I am reliving these difficult memories, it feels like it all happened yesterday. But in reality, it's been two decades. Life is good now, pretty peaceful, and has been for a long time. We've been in a period of such harmony, in fact, that it feels a bit like the universe is trying to balance the scales. I don't know if that's true, but I'll take it. I'm healthy. My career is back on track. I have a wonderful marriage, and my two sons—including the one who doctors said I should never have carried to term because of my illness—are thriving, grown men.

With life rolling along well and this book coming out, the sad part of this story sometimes feels like it happened a million years ago. Either way, what I can never do is forget everything that I've learned from my experiences of tragedy and triumph—specifically, that no matter how hard I've been knocked down, and no matter how dire the threat to our lives, I have fought like a champion. I have mustered the courage to fight the battle again and again. Though I have often been scared, angry, and frustrated, I didn't run and I didn't quit. I won. I found a champion in myself that I never knew existed until I was tested.

Every book needs a mission, and this is mine: to share my hard-won life lessons and offer hope to others who may face adversity that they fear they can't handle. If you're in that situation, know this: *You can handle it.* You have a champion in you. We all do. You can rise to the challenges you face—and if you open yourself up to other people, they will come from the most unlikely places to help you. Most important, there is a design, a destiny behind it all. It might not be the path you envisioned for your life, but that's not something you can control. As one of my favorite quotes says, "Life is 10 percent how we make it and 90 percent how we take it." I didn't think I could take it like a champion, but I did. And so can you.

All that said, it's time to let you discover the whole story yourself. So let me take you back to Philadelphia, Pennsylvania, in 1986 and introduce you to a sweet, marvelous little girl named Lauren who changed my world forever.

Birth

"What was that?"

Did I imagine that quick, sharp pain in my abdomen? Or did I inadvertently twist my torso in my sleep? I look at the clock—4:00 a.m. Hmm . . . maybe this is the start of my long-awaited labor. Or maybe it's just another annoying muscle spasm. Better try to get some sleep regardless. If this is "my time," I've probably got a long haul ahead of me in the hours to come.

I've heard repeatedly that first-time labor is usually long and exhausting. My husband, Jim, and I expect to put in no less than eight to ten hours of labor; my excellent health and up-until-now perfect pregnancy apparently don't count for much. All the "first-timers" in our childbirth class had lengthy labors that required pain medication. I groan at the prospect. On the other hand, it will be great to get rid of some of these extra fifty pounds I've been carrying.

There were eight couples in our childbirth preparation group. Ruth and I are the slackers, the ones yet to deliver. Ruth's due date is the latest, and I'm a week past my date. It figures. I myself was born a week late, to the dismay of my parents. It was especially inconvenient because my dad, an active serviceman, had specifically obtained the week of my anticipated birth off, but had to return to duty before I was born. But I've always been a perfectionist, so I often take more time to accomplish tasks—including gestation, apparently.

I drift back to sleep thinking about the past year. Jim and I are thrilled to finally be starting our family. We married young (I was only twenty-one) after being high school and college sweethearts, but we decided not to have children right away. We both grew up with solid, middle-class parents who valued a good home and quality education, and we wanted to "work our way up" to financial security before starting a family. We didn't want to struggle like the couples of our parents' generation, who were expected have a bun in the oven within months of "I do"—resulting in a one-income family and financial constraints.

That was eight years ago, and the time has flown. We've been busy with our jobs, the lovely home that we bought, our family, our friends, and travel. With our combined seven siblings, numerous cousins, and many friends, life has been a blur of weddings, showers, christenings, and birthday parties. But almost a year ago, at twenty-nine, I felt my biological alarm clock go off and say, "Don't forget about me." Call it maternal instinct, but I knew it was the right time for me to become pregnant. We were finally in the financial position to start a family.

I've been an achiever since age fourteen, when I was able to start babysitting and earn some spending money. During my college years, I sometimes I took on two jobs in the summer to help pay for my tuition, clothes, auto expenses, and, of course, some occasional entertainment. A true Capricorn, I'm a worker. Now I'm a financial advisor—in a high-turnover, low-retention business in which women are a "statistical minority." But I've muscled through to climb the ladders of achievement at work, and this year, I was awarded the President's Cabinet award, the second-highest sales award within our company. I chuckle on my pillow as I think how absurd I must have looked a month and a half ago at our annual agency awards banquet and ceremony in Atlantic City, standing onstage and in the spotlight alongside our tuxedoed top executives with a full-blown pregnancy belly.

No one has asked me about my plans for coming back to work after the baby's born. I suppose they're all thinking, "At least she's going out on top." But I have every intention of continuing my career, albeit, perhaps, at a slower pace.

❋ ❋

It's been a joyous nine months for us. I am thrilled that this is my time to become a mother. Throughout pregnancy, my health has been excellent, and I have truly never felt happier in my entire life. We've had a lot of fun preparing these past months in anticipation of James Joseph Barker IV, if he's a boy, or Lauren Barker, if she's a girl. We chose the boy's name to honor Jim's family, especially his charismatic grandpop, who passed away two years ago. I chose Lauren for a girl's name simply because I love the sound of it, the beauty that it evokes. I am not yet certain about a middle name. I have considered my own name, Elizabeth; it flows well with Lauren. We'll decide when we meet the baby.

I enjoy decorating, so it was a joy to create a unisex nursery with a pastel color scheme of pale yellow and green. We purchased a nice oak crib, dresser, changing table, and rocker, expecting that they will serve us not only for this baby but also our subsequent children. Initially, though, our newborn infant won't sleep in that room—we have the old-fashioned rocking cradle that Jim's mom bought for her firstborn grandchild, my three-year-old nephew, set up next to our bed. Our baby will be the second temporary owner of this special cradle. All the precious, tiny baby clothes we have are tucked neatly in the dresser drawers, and the changing table is stocked with diapers and accessories. My hospital bag is packed and waiting for its call of duty. The house is clean. The bills are paid. My job responsibilities are under control. Everything is ready as we wait for Baby Barker to be born.

We have no idea what our baby's sex is. We made the perennial parental wish—"a healthy child"—and left it at that.

At our last childbirth preparation class, Mary, the instructor, had us participate in an unusual group activity. She passed around a bowl containing small pieces of folded paper. She said that each one had a "thought-provoking and challenging question" on it regarding the birth process. Each couple picked a slip, read it aloud to the class, and gave their honest response.

The questions were about birth situations that might deviate from our expectations or from a routine birthing experience. Some hypothetical questions dealt with the dignity of the birth process. One was about the need for pain medication despite the goal of natural childbirth. Others were about having an unexpected C-section or extraordinarily long or complicated labor incidents.

The question on the slip of paper that Jim and I picked:

How would you react if your baby was born with a health problem, genetic issue, or a disability?

Obviously, this is something no parent wants to think about. We had not discussed birth defects or serious labor and delivery problems in the class, and this had never really crossed Jim's or my mind. My pregnancy had been textbook perfect so far, and neither of our families had any genetic problems. My only fear was getting through the birthing process without too much wear and tear (literally). But we had to come up with an answer.

When our turn came, I could see the change of expression on everyone's face. The levity left the room. All eyes were on us to see how we'd answer this question. But our response was noncommittal: "It would naturally be a huge disappointment after all of our years of anticipation and recent months of preparation." What else could we say?

"It's important to understand that there can sometimes be unexpected issues during the birth process, or with the health of a newborn," our instructor said after we gave our answer.

No one engaged or followed up with any questions. None of us wanted her to elaborate; none of us wanted to hear anything more about it. It was too deep and too scary, especially since everyone appeared so healthy. So we moved on from that exercise, and the last class closed joyously. We were all giddy with excitement and anticipation of our due dates in the upcoming few weeks. We had set up a phone chain to keep track of our births, and a reunion was planned for us to get together with our babies a short while after all of our deliveries. Jim and I went home in a blissful state that night. We were looking forward to a happy new chapter of our lives together, and to sharing it with new people with whom we hoped we'd be lifelong friends.

Ouch—another sharp pain in my abdomen brings me out of this dreamy state. Oh well, it's time for my usual middle-of-the-night trip to the bathroom anyway. I don't mind this now-routine 4:00 a.m. awakening. My body has become used to interrupted sleep. I figure it's good training for nighttime feedings. But this time, I'm passing a lot of fluid, along with mucus and some faint blood. As I peer into the toilet bowl trying to figure out if I've dropped the infamous "mucus plug," a long, sharp pain hits me.

This is it! My long-overdue labor has begun! My thoughts begin to race: *What will my experience be like? Will it be long and painful? Will I need medications or surgical repair? What if an emergency C-section is called for? Will we have a baby boy, as we're hoping for?*

I head back to my bed to try to get some sleep. I pull out my lighted watch to help me keep track of the contractions, and it doesn't take long to establish a regular, lengthy pattern. By 6:00 a.m. I've made several trips to the bathroom and it's clear that the contractions are getting stronger and closer together. I wake Jim. After he dresses and makes coffee, my water breaks.

We rush to the hospital, just ten minutes away. That dark, heavy question from our last birth class is the last thing on my mind.

I am wheeled up to the maternity floor and instructed to put on one of those skimpy hospital gowns. At this point, well into heavy contractions, I could care less about how I look. I feel as if I am in a zone or state of lethargy in between contractions. We are pleased that the comfortable and pleasant birthing room is available to us instead of the usual cold, sterile hospital delivery room.

I manage to get up on the delivery table and lie back for my initial exam.

The nurse exclaims, "Oh my goodness, I can see the head of the baby and he/she has lots of hair!" She starts to fire statements and questions rapidly:

"Congratulations, you are fully dilated at stage 10 and ready to deliver.

"I need to get the doctor in here as soon as possible for you, don't push yet.

"How long were you in labor at home?

"Why did you wait so long to come in?"

Jim and I explain that I was only in labor for a short while at home, and that it hasn't even been that difficult for me. Even in my stupor, I'm beaming. *Wow, am I lucky! No one we know has ever told such an easy birth story.* I feel relaxed, almost sedated, though I have been given no medication. I actually catnap in between my contractions and the hard pushing. I feel proud that my body is "performing" so well.

The doctor is with us constantly now. He is perched on a stool at the foot of my gurney waiting for the next wave of contractions and pushes. He tells me that I will need an episiotomy because the baby is large: at least nine pounds. Yikes! Jim is six foot one, but I am only five foot four and petite. I avoid thinking about the logistics; I just focus on the doctor's instructions.

After the episiotomy, the fetal monitor attached to the baby's head starts to beep abnormally. Visions of a tangled umbilical cord run through my head. *Damn, I knew this was too good to be true.* I turn on my right side and then my left, but still the machine beeps, indicating a continuing problem.

I know that I am not thinking straight at this point—I am in the end stages of heavy labor—but I ask, "What the hell is going on?"

Jim looks scared. No one answers my question. Is it because they don't know? Fifteen minutes ago, the doctor was commenting on what an easy birth this is turning out to be. Now his face looks grim.

Suddenly, everything is changing. I'm whisked from the small, quiet birthing room to a huge, cold operating room rapidly filling with medical staff and equipment. There are bright, blaring lights shining down on me now—a stark contrast to the cozy atmosphere

I've grown used to over the past couple of hours. I figure that I am too far along for a C-section now. How could my experience have gone from dream to nightmare so suddenly? Most of all I wonder, *How is my baby?*

The doctor explains that the baby's heartbeat is becoming strained and weaker; he urges me to give the next contraction my best and biggest push in order to get the baby out. I brace my arms on the metal bed and push with all my strength and a hefty scream. I hear a pop and then I feel a tremendous release. I flop back on the pillow, spent and drowsy.

"Congratulations, Liz and Jim, you have a baby girl," the doctor announces. "And she is a big baby, too!"

They swaddle her in a soft blanket and bring her to me, but I feel so spent and sleepy that I can barely keep my eyes open. Jim holds her for me because my arms are too weak to do it. I look her over and smile at her pudgy round face. But after a minute, my smile fades.

Something is not right. Why is she so still? Her eyes are closed. *Why is she not crying or screaming? And what kind of horrid new mother am I, looking at my precious new baby with apprehension? My brain must be scrambled from labor.* I try to focus and examine her more closely.

She seems a little dusky in color—kind of blue. The nurse is holding an oxygen tube under her nose. I recall reading in my childbirth book that bigger babies are sometimes born with a bluish color. She is definitely big: nine pounds fourteen point five ounces and twenty-one inches. It's a family record! *That big, she's got to be healthy,* I think. Still, despite my fogginess, I sense that something is not quite right.

They have taken our daughter from Jim and are in an adjacent room with her. The nurse explains that they are taking her to the nursery for some blood tests and to keep an oxygen mask on her until she gains some color. If I weren't so tired, I would ask more questions. Jim seems satisfied with the vague answers we're getting, and I don't have the energy to disagree. I fall asleep after asking him for reassurance. He leaves the room to use the phone and announce our daughter's birth. We still haven't agreed on her name.

My dozing is interrupted by the doctor twisting my abdomen to release the afterbirth and then giving me stitches. Because I am so groggy, I don't notice that he is not upbeat or chatty with me about this happy event.

"There is a call in to your new pediatrician," the doctor tells us when Jim returns. "We'll let you know when we hear back from him."

I chose this pediatrician upon recommendation from my OB practice doctors. We've never actually met the man. We did not anticipate anything unusual about our newborn or his/her health, so we didn't think to "interview" a pediatrician ahead of time.

"As soon as we have your baby's oxygen reading at the desired level, the nurses will bring her to you," the doctor promises.

With his reassuring statement, I breathe a sigh of relief and allow myself to doze again. I have never experienced birth before, therefore I assume that what the medical staff is doing and telling us is par for the course. I don't know any better. I trust that the doctor is always right. And in my state of fatigue, I'm not alert enough to fully comprehend or suspect that something is seriously wrong with our daughter. With such an easy birth and with her nice size and weight, I'd be silly to worry.

After I am cleaned up and stitched up, I am wheeled into my maternity room. After a short snooze there, I feel refreshed. I wake up alert, excited about our birth, and anxious to see my precious baby girl. I am longing to hold and bond with her and to try to breast-feed her.

A nurse comes in, and I ask her about having my daughter in the room with us so that we can begin our bonding process. Our childbirth classes covered the importance of immediate physical bonding with your newborn.

She leaves to check.

Then both sets of our parents arrive, joyful and bearing flowers. Ours is the first granddaughter in the family. Jim walks them to the nursery to look for our baby. Although she is not in the nursery window yet, they do meet the new pediatrician there, on his way to see us.

When he enters my room, he appears somber. We sense that something may be wrong. My joy suddenly vanishes, and a sense of dread sets in. With Jim holding my hand bedside and our parents surrounding us, we wait for what's to come, bracing ourselves for bad news.

"I just examined your daughter," he tells us, "and I have some preliminary news.

"She was blue at birth due to a lack of oxygen, which I suspect is the result of a serious heart defect," he says. "Unfortunately, treating this sort of defect is beyond my capabilities and beyond the scope of Phoenician General Hospital. Your baby needs specialized care at a pediatric hospital as soon as possible. I have already called for her immediate transport via ambulance to William Penn Memorial Hospital in North Philadelphia."

Without missing a beat, he continues. "I recommend that you formally name her and informally baptize her here in your room when they wheel her in for a brief visit before she is taken to the ambulance," he says matter-of-factly. Then he exits the room.

We're all stunned. Horrified. I turn to Jim, and everyone bursts out sobbing. My gut has known that something is wrong since the moment I saw our sweet baby, and now my mind starts spinning as my visions of a perfect beginning to our family life sputter and go dark. *How could this happen to us? We've done all the right things! Neither of our families has any history of serious health problems or birth defects. I was so careful during my pregnancy!*

I think about the idiotic women who drink or smoke during their pregnancies and yet somehow have perfectly healthy babies. This makes me furious. *Why me? Why is God punishing me? I worked so hard, planned so carefully—I wanted this baby so badly!*

"It's not fair!" I scream. I am so sad that my poor baby girl is being torn away from us and we haven't even been able to hold her or cuddle her. I am so afraid of what will happen next when she is taken away.

A nurse and the transport team arrive in my room with my

baby girl asleep in the sealed oxygen incubator. I burst into tears again. She looks so pitiful as she sleeps. The love and pain I feel are almost more than I can bear. My arms desperately want to hold my daughter and give her my warmth, but she is locked away from us, enclosed in a sterile glass box where I can't even touch her. I feel sick.

Someone from the staff opens the lid of her incubator bed, hands me a small cup of water, and asks me to baptize our daughter. I have to decide on the name *now*. With a shaky hand, I pour some water on her head to confirm that her name will be Lauren Elizabeth Barker. I sob pitifully as I pray aloud and beg God to protect and heal our precious daughter. The fact that I have given her my name provides me with some comfort. It feels like I have given her a part of myself to go with her to the new hospital. I reach into the incubator and touch her tiny baby hand to say good-bye as I tear up again.

Jim rides with Lauren in the ambulance to the hospital. His parents follow in their car so they can support and be with him there. Because of Lauren's large size, my episiotomy and other birth trauma render it too painful for me to move or walk. I am left feeling like a train wreck both physically and emotionally. I am not ready to face the world yet. My parents stay to comfort me. As the day passes, they will make the same exhausting phone call over and over, explaining to family and friends what has happened and what little we know.

From Dream to Nightmare

After several hours of visiting, comforting, and calls, my weary parents decide to head home to rest. I promise to keep them updated. Jim has been phoning me periodically these past few hours with bits of information. Finally, we receive the diagnosis and the bad news.

Preliminary tests indicate that Lauren has a serious heart defect called atrioventricular canal and tetralogy of Fallot. The four chambers of her heart are not normal, and one is leaking blood. This is what caused her listlessness and her dusky color at birth. My poor baby was literally fighting for her life at the moment of her birth.

The doctors told Jim, upon his arrival at William Penn Memorial, that Lauren's potentially lethal heart defect required immediate surgical repair, with a shunt to reroute the blood flow so that her heart will be able process oxygen correctly. Without surgery, they said, she will die. Jim, supported by his more clear-headed parents, consented. The surgery took place immediately and was expected to take approximately three hours. The surgery is over now, but it will take many hours of watching and waiting to determine its effectiveness. There is nothing to do but to wait.

Thankfully, the nursing staff has had the sense not to put another woman in my room. I don't think I would be able to handle it if they did. After the shock and trauma I've experienced today, seeing a happy new mother in my room with her healthy newborn would give me an emotional breakdown. I would be consumed with envy, rage, and sadness, thinking *That should have been me, that should have been me,* over and over again. It would not be a pleasant situation for anyone.

My sister-in-law, Linda, calls with some reassurance for me: her nephew in Florida was born with a severe heart defect eleven years ago and is fine now. I had forgotten about him. But now I remember that I met the little boy, Ricky, at their wedding in Florida two years ago. He was a perfectly normal, active preteen who liked to show off his chest scar. The reminder of his success in spite of his rough start makes me feel a little better.

At about 8:00 p.m., Jim calls, sounding exhausted and stressed. The surgery is over and has been deemed successful—so far. But there's a long way to go. Lauren is in the neonatal intensive care unit (NICU) resting peacefully. Jim is heading back to Phoenician General to give me more details in person. Between Linda's call about Ricky and Jim's call about the success of the surgery, I felt better and more optimistic. I rationalize that Lauren's size and weight are in her favor, and since her heart surgery went well, the worst of it is over. Now we simply need to pray for her recovery. Feeling physically and emotionally battered, but somewhat reassured, I fall asleep as soon as I hang up with Jim.

I wake upon his arrival and I'm startled by his appearance. It is obvious that he has been crying. His eyes are bloodshot and his face is puffy and red. My stomach drops. He climbs onto the bed with me and hugs me fiercely.

"There is more about Lauren," he says before breaking into sobs.

"What is it?" I cry. "What's wrong? Whatever it is, we can handle it together."

Jim composes himself and tells me that Lauren's heart condition is a symptom of Down syndrome. Our beautiful baby isn't just physically impaired—she's also mentally retarded.

The words Jim is speaking make no sense. I've never heard of Down syndrome. I understand mental retardation but have no idea what causes it to occur in newborns. I think that perhaps a traumatic birth could cause it, especially if a baby was deprived of oxygen. I immediately think about how the fetal monitor was beeping and how we were whisked away to the operating room for

Lauren's delivery. Is that why she has Down syndrome? Because she couldn't get enough oxygen?

"No," Jim explains. "It was definitely not the labor or delivery. This isn't your fault," he says. "And it's not anyone else's, either. It just is."

As I will later learn all too well, Down syndrome is a chromosomal abnormality usually involving an extra copy of chromosome 21 in either the egg or sperm cell. This is called trisomy 21. Most conceptions that result from either an egg or a sperm carrying an extra chromosome result in early miscarriage. Those that don't abort produce a baby with some type of mental retardation. The abnormality happened randomly when either the egg or sperm was formed. Because women have all their eggs at birth, the older a woman is at conception, the greater the risk of abnormalities such as Down syndrome. That is why genetic testing is recommended for women who conceive at age thirty-five or older.

Because I'm only twenty-nine, experienced a near-perfect pregnancy, and have no family history of fetal or genetic disorders, there was no reason for me to have genetic testing. There has never been an indication that the baby that I was carrying had health problems. Lauren's fetal heartbeats in utero were always normal.

The knowledge that this wasn't our fault doesn't ease our pain and fear, however. Nobody we know has delivered a baby with health issues, so we have no idea what to expect. Perhaps we lived in a sheltered world or perhaps no one talks about the bad experiences, but we honestly cannot recall any family member, friend, or acquaintance whose baby has been born with a long-term health condition. Yes, we know of instances of jaundice, slight premature birth due to placenta problems, and several miscarriages, but never anything life threatening like this.

After just one hour, my temporary sense of calm and optimism about Lauren has vanished. Round two has now begun, starting with this sucker punch of more bad news. I'm realizing that the reality is, even when Lauren recovers from this surgery, she will be handicapped for life with her mental disability. There is no cure. It is what it is.

The only exposure I've had to a child with mental retardation was when I was in elementary school. A little girl who lived in my neighborhood, Pammy, had some sort of mental handicap. Pammy's mother was a single mom who liked to drink, it was rumored. Pammy and her sister always looked unkempt—messy hair, shabby clothes. Pammy also seemed to have a perpetually snotty nose. We all wondered if the girls' mother's drinking was the cause of Pammy's retardation or the result of her trying to cope with it.

Remembering Pammy, I determine right here and now that our Lauren will not be like her. Our daughter, whatever her condition might be, will not be ridiculed or treated in a condescending manner, the way Pammy was. And I will never behave like Pammy's broken-down mother.

Suddenly, I also recall Mary Lou. I was friends with her sister, Pat. Mary Lou was the youngest of eight children. She had physical and mental disabilities. Pat's dad was a very successful attorney, and whenever I visited the family's beautiful home, Pat's mom always seemed polished and professional. She was obviously well educated, she dressed impeccably, and she spoke to everyone, including all of her children and their guests, with grace and courtesy. Unlike Pammy's pitiful mom, she never appeared angry, frustrated, or out of sorts. And Pat and her siblings had obviously been brought up to not be ashamed of Mary Lou. Rather than focus on her disabilities, they all celebrated her abilities.

That's how I will raise my daughter, I promise myself. *I will offer that same loving and inclusive experience to my Lauren, no matter what it takes.*

After talking and crying for hours, Jim and I fall asleep in each other's arms. In the middle of the night, Jim creeps into the other bed in my room and we sleep for a while longer, spent by our emotional ordeal. But at 7:00 a.m., a harsh nurse with a nasty disposition strolls in and immediately snarls at Jim about sleeping in the other bed.

"What if we needed that bed? Now we have to change it!" she snaps. "The hospital may charge you for this."

What a witch, I think. *Doesn't she know the hell we've been through in the past twenty-four hours—that we are physical and emotional wrecks?* I thought nurses were supposed to be compassionate. It wasn't like we've been up all night celebrating and drinking champagne.

"We're sorry," I whimper back while actually wanting to scream, "but we needed to be together for support."

She coldly runs through what she needs to do with me, then takes my temperature and blood pressure. When she's done, she leaves, without even a single a word of compassion.

I will learn soon that the medical field is populated with plenty of people like her—people more concerned with exercising authority or having their routine followed than with truly caring for patients. We will encounter several of them in the near future. But for now, I assume she is an exception to the rule.

Jim and I decide to get me the hell out of that hospital as soon as possible, both to avoid having to share my room with another new mother and to avoid dealing with anyone else like that nurse. When one of the team of doctors comes in to see me, he agrees to discharge me immediately, understanding my predicament. But I am not yet well enough to go to William Penn Memorial to see Lauren. I need to go someplace quiet to rest. My body is still throbbing from the delivery and the ensuing stitches. I have hemorrhoids from pushing. My mind is scrambled and foggy. I haven't fully mentally and emotionally processed the news about Lauren.

Because one of us needs to be at William Penn Memorial for the first few days after Lauren's surgery, we decide that we will stay at my parents' home for a while. Our home in Phoenixville is an hour from Philadelphia. My parents' home is much closer. I also can't face being alone and far away from family support right now. I fear going back to my bedroom and that empty cradle sitting next to our bed, and I dread seeing the beautiful baby nursery that we so lovingly set up. Both of these will remind me that my fairy-tale dreams about my firstborn and our much-anticipated homecoming are now shattered.

After discharge, Jim and I part. He heads to the pediatric hospital in the city to visit Lauren. My parents take me home so I can pick up clothes and things for the next few days. Though my dad thoughtfully tries to intercept me and remove the cradle before I enter the room, I see it. I break down and sob for a moment, but then say, "Leave it, Dad. What's the sense of moving it elsewhere? It doesn't change what's happened."

I am already channeling my inner Pat's mom, striving to stay logical and in control. Drama and tantrums serve no purpose. I will cry because I am sad, but I will not go crazy. I need to be as strong as I can be for my baby. I feel a bit numb at this point. So that helps.

On the ride to my parents' house, I reflect on the past twenty-four hours. In minutes, my life has completely and forever changed. All of our careful plans, cultivated for years, have been smashed. Our dream has become a nightmare. The joyous expectations of the past nine months now seem like self-delusion. I feel like my life has been taken from me. I don't want to see or speak with anyone other than close family. I feel raw inside. Until I can come to terms with what has happened in the hours since Lauren's birth, I won't be able to explain it to anyone else.

During this time of reflection and respite in my old bedroom at my parents' home, another memory comes back. It's something that happened in January, just three months prior to Lauren's birth. As part of the award I won at work, I was given a long weekend trip to the Bahamas. *Perfect,* I had thought. It would be nice to go somewhere sunny and relaxing after the busy holidays, and it was right around my twenty-ninth birthday.

On our first day on the Bahamas' Paradise Island, Jim and I were walking along the streets of the straw market shopping area and I tripped on one of the many broken old sidewalks—at six months, I had a big belly that often made me feel awkward and clumsy. As I pitched forward, an elderly native woman near me caught my arm to help break my fall.

"Thank you," I said sincerely, and our eyes met.

She stared intensely at me in a peculiar way and said, "You don't look older than thirty-five; are you?"

Wow, what kind of a question is that to ask another woman? I found it especially odd because people always think I'm much younger than I am. But she had just helped me, so I didn't want to be rude: I mumbled no, that I was only twenty-nine, and then I hurried on my way.

That strange chance encounter lasted all of twenty seconds. I thought nothing of it at the time. But now, as it came back to me out of the blue, I wondered: *Did that woman have intuition or psychic ability? Did she see or sense that the baby that I was carrying was handicapped? Is that why she thought that I might be older—because she knew that I was carrying a child with Down syndrome?* Suddenly I have goose bumps.

I think back about the question that Jim and I had serendipitously picked at that last childbirth class—the one that asked, "What would you do if your child was born with a health problem or handicap?" Was that, too, a sign? A warning of what might happen in my future? Perhaps both of these incidents were "angel moments," the universe telling me to stop and think. But I blissfully ignored them. I was so confident of my good health and my family's history that I ignored these hints of foretelling.

This is a wake-up call. I resolve that going forward, I will be more receptive to any mystical moments I encounter and more willing to trust my instincts. I know that the three of us—especially Lauren—have a long, hard road ahead. I need to be strong and present for her to survive and thrive. Keeping my eyes, ears, and mind open will help me do just that.

After a day of sedated rest at my parents' home, I feel well enough to venture with them and Jim to William Penn Memorial to see Lauren. The hospital is located in one of the worst neighborhoods of North Philadelphia. To get there, we drive through a severely blighted neighborhood nicknamed the Badlands by police due to its notorious drug trafficking. On my future drives through this area, I will marvel that the struggling people who inhabit this area seemed to give birth to healthy children easily, despite their poverty and drug use. Again I will question why I—so careful, living such a clean and sober life—have had a baby who must suffer so much.

William Penn Memorial is depressing—dismal, old, located in that terrible neighborhood. There is no visitor parking lot, and we are nervous about parking our car on the street. We are unfamiliar with big, urban teaching hospitals that serious health conditions demand. But we are about to encounter some harsh lessons on the mind-boggling realities of the medical and health insurance industries. By the time all is said and done, we'll know more about this world than we ever wanted.

Survival Tactics

William Penn Memorial's interior doesn't look much better than its exterior. I feel overdressed compared to everyone else, even in my now-baggy maternity clothes. Stress has robbed me of my appetite, and because Lauren is my first child, my maternity weight and water weight are disappearing fast. That is the only positive aspect of my postpartum life so far.

I begin to wonder why my new pediatrician made the decision for our baby to come to this depressing hospital. I know it is supposed to have a renowned pediatric cardiac unit, but don't we have excellent health insurance? Shouldn't we be able to go somewhere nicer than this?

I have been a wage earner since age sixteen, paying income and Social Security taxes, and for seven of the eight years that Jim and I have been married, up until the beginning of this year, I paid for a traditional medical insurance plan that had a modest deductible and an eighty/twenty co-pay schedule up to a certain amount per year.

This January, however—four months before Lauren was born—I decided to change our medical plan to an HMO, inspired by discussions with coworkers who have young children and who told me that an HMO offered them much lower co-payments, especially for the expected multiple pediatric doctor visits and immunizations. They convinced me that it would be far less expensive for me to have an HMO plan with young children. With no frame of reference, I switched. I understood that this would narrow my physician choices and also require referrals to speak to specialists, but that didn't seem like such a big deal. *Jim and I are so healthy,* I thought. *I won't have to worry about those details.*

But it is our new HMO plan, with its many cost-control restrictions, that has caused us to end up at dismal William Penn Memorial instead of the renowned Children's Hospital of Pennsylvania, located in the prestigious University City area of Philadelphia. What I will soon learn is that the lower costs of HMOs make them more attractive, but the reality is, they are primarily designed for people who are well. If you are older, have someone in your family with a chronic health condition, or have a child with special needs, an HMO is probably not your best bet. I'm learning my first huge lesson regarding health insurance: never assume that perfect health remains indefinitely. It is wiser to choose a plan that will offer you the best benefits when you need them most, not one that will only serve you well when you are in optimal health.

I have to wash my hands and don a protective hospital gown over our street clothes prior to entering the fourth-floor NICU. The room contains a dizzying array of medical equipment, arranged as several tall columns that serve as power and equipment resource cores. Jutting out from each of these core columns like spokes of a wheel are three high-tech baby beds for ill newborns. It looks like the suspended animation scene at the beginning of *Alien*.

The babies in these beds are sleeping, bandaged, frail-looking things with little or no clothes on. Heat lamps are positioned above them, and they all have multiple intravenous lines. Monitors keep track of their vitals. It is a frightening and abnormal scene, far different from looking at the lovely, healthy newborns swaddled in pink or blue in the maternity ward. No one expects to face this scenario with her newborn. No one thinks she'll end up here.

Feeling sick at the sight of all this, I brace myself for what Lauren will look like. I remember how she looked on the day of her birth—her head full of dark, wavy hair—but mostly because the thoughtful paramedics took a Polaroid of her that they kindly handed to us before they whisked her off in the ambulance. I've stared at the picture many times in the past two days. When I arrive at her bedside, however, I am horrified by what I see, and I burst out crying. She is nothing like the blanket-swaddled baby in the Polaroid. This Lauren is naked, and her body is covered head to toe with bandages, sticky monitor pads, and IVs. She is on a ventilator, and her bed is a clear, enclosed capsule with temperature and oxygen controls.

I cry for her, not me. I worry that she is in pain despite her sedation. Most of all, I think, *What must this poor baby be thinking?* She came into this world literally gasping for breath and was barely held and cuddled before being whisked away by strangers, only to be poked, prodded, cut, and intubated. Her only nourishment has come from a feeding tube—a thought that reminds me of my pent-up breast milk, which has made my breasts sore and rock hard. I realize that no one has counseled me about pumping or storing my breast milk. I wonder if the doctors are not optimistic about Lauren's chance of survival, or if there are simply much more serious issues to cope with first.

When I calm down, I turn to Jim. "Are we doing the right thing?" I ask him. "Or are we putting our child through physical torture for no reason?"

He has no answer for me.

I don't know the scenarios and choices related to medicine and ethics for Lauren's case. Are we, along with her doctors, making medical decisions that will save her only temporarily? Is she in excruciating pain? Who is ultimately responsible for making such decisions? Is it our choice, or does the hospital administration supersede us? I need answers to so many questions:

What is the extent of her heart defect?
When will we know if the surgery was successful?
Will she need more surgery in the future?
Will she have a chance for a normal life?

Later, we will learn that babies with Down syndrome face health challenges that "normal" babies do not. They have weak muscle tone, which can lead to difficulty with breathing, eating, and healing after surgery; their condition can handicap their recovery time and reduce the odds of positive outcomes. Because of this, in this moment, no one, including our doctors, has any answers yet. They have done their best to repair her heart defect with a shunt, but beyond that, they can't do much. At this point, the priority is putting out fires.

After we've spent some time with Lauren, her cardiologist, Dr. Ronald Dawson, sits down to talk with us. He explains that the hospital's ethics committee will review Lauren's case tomorrow and make decisions about the suggested course of her care. Dr. Dawson seems like a sincere, compassionate man whose advice I can rely on. I decide to trust my instincts and place my faith in him. Jim and I resolve to wait for his and the committee's evaluations.

For today, I sit on a high stool and gaze at my baby, talking softly to her and touching her hand or arm through one of the bed's side pockets. I also silently pray for her. I want her to live if it is best for her, but my heart will break if we put her through all this only to give her a short life full of pain. Sitting there, touching her tiny hand, I feel that I am building our bond despite our lack of full physical contact.

From this day on, my life will never again be the same. We have entered a new world order of medical, insurance, and special needs issues. This is our life now.

I'm entitled to my six weeks of maternity leave with pay, and I take them. What will happen after that? There are a myriad of unanswerable questions to cope with. For now, our days are a run-on of the following schedule: I arrive at the hospital each morning and stay all day; Jim joins me after work for a bit; then one set of our parents relieves us for the "late shift."

We all share the feeling that Lauren is helpless and needs us to watch over her—and with good reason. This is a teaching hospital, and the array of doctors, specialists, therapists, social workers, and aspiring doctors is mind boggling. I gradually learn the difference between med students, residents, interns, fellows, and the like—the various components of the doctor hierarchy. It seems like there is always someone stopping by to examine Lauren, read her chart, and poke and prod her.

I have a sixth sense about people, and I learn to distinguish the wonderful and compassionate individuals from the rest in these roving packs of medical personnel. I begin to resent the ones—especially the students and interns—who are cold and indifferent. *Are you becoming a doctor for the money and status,* I want to ask some of them, *or have you always been pompous and pretentious?* I draw comfort from the specialty nurses of this NICU, who are uniformly dedicated and caring. They are especially kind and compassionate to my family, I think because they see our own dedication to being with and supporting Lauren.

Still, it is difficult to get detailed, quality information about Lauren's status. With so many attending specialists—cardiac, respiratory, etc.—I often wonder, *Who is the real "quarterback" of all of this? Who is coordinating and making decisions about the various aspects of Lauren's care?* We get bits and pieces of information if we are lucky enough to be present when the specialists stop by, but nothing comprehensive—nothing that truly helps us understand her situation. And it's difficult to find the strength to ask for more. We are so overwhelmed by the complexity of Lauren's condition and our own emotional and physical exhaustion that we're numb. We are taking it day by day, hanging on for dear life. We don't yet know how to advocate for ourselves or our daughter.

A few days after the surgery, we meet with Dr. Dawson again. He informs us that the medical team and ethics committee consider Lauren's surgery to have been successful. She will need similar surgery in the future to keep up with her growing body's needs, but that likely won't be until she is about three years old. For now, she is progressing and healing.

"The next step is to wean her from the ventilator," he tells us. "But that's tricky with Down syndrome babies, because they tend to have narrow airways and weak muscle tone in the throat. And Lauren has been heavily sedated all this time, which will make weaning even more challenging."

I hear what he's saying, and I worry that this process will be frightening, and possibly painful, for Lauren. But I also think of how nice it will be to have her breathing on her own and to see her face clearly, without the tubes and tape. *She can have a more normal baby bed once she's off the ventilator,* I think, *and get out of that stupid plastic incubator.* I let myself feel excited about that prospect.

As the days wear on, we are introduced to a social worker named Karen. I immediately like her; she seems caring and really wants to help us. She arranges for us to meet two sets of parents—Diane and Steve Otter and Pat and Dave Patterson—who live in our suburban area, are about our age, and have preschool-age daughters with Down syndrome. Like Lauren, their daughters had medical conditions that warranted immediate surgery after birth.

Both of these couples have been through (and survived) what we are now experiencing. They and their daughters are thriving. We speak over the phone a few times, and then Pat is gracious enough to invite me to come to her home to meet her, Dave, and their daughter, Jillian. She also invites me to shadow her for a day as she juggles her routine with Jillian at her special needs preschool and the flex job that her employer has granted her.

After spending a half day with Pat and Jillian, I feel comforted and optimistic about our futures. Pat is warm and kind. She reminds me a great deal of my prior self when I felt more assured and in control of my life. She offers me hope that one day I, too, will be able to cope with my dramatic changes. Life will go on, albeit in a new world order. Two-year-old Jillian amazes me as well. I am impressed with how vibrant and healthy she is despite her rough beginning at birth. Like Lauren, she needed major surgery on her birth day because of a severe gastrointestinal abnormality. You'd never know it now, seeing her running around like any other toddler. Meeting Pat and Jillian that day was a huge turning point for me. It made me realize that my life would not have to be like that of Pammy's mom, that it was up to me to make our lives the best that they could be, regardless of any handicaps. Although we didn't know what the future held for us, I felt that a huge weight of uncertainty was lifted that day.

My work situation has been on my mind these weeks, in part because our health insurance benefits come solely through my employment. I can't afford to lose my job. Luckily, Pat is a great mentor; I am encouraged by her ability to multitask. *I can do this,* I think. And I mostly believe it.

Back at the hospital, the respiratory people have been unsuccessful at weaning Lauren off the ventilator. The attempts seem traumatizing for her, and we are getting mixed messages and misinformation about the process. Once again, we're on edge.

"If we can't get her to breathe on her own soon," Dr. Dawson tells us, "we will have to do a tracheotomy."

They want to cut a hole in my daughter's throat? I've seen the babies who have gotten tracheotomies—the short breathing tubes attached with a string around their necks, like a bizarre, ugly choker. I don't want this for her. But in the end, I don't really have a say: weaning fails, and the tracheotomy becomes necessary. This is not only a devastating setback, but it will have significant repercussions in the near future. After three weeks of sadness, grief, anger, confusion, and gloom, we wearily consent to the surgery with the hopes that it will give Lauren the opportunity to progress with her recovery and that we will finally be able to hold and cuddle her. We ache to hold our daughter. We are sure that contact with us will enhance her healing.

And happily, the procedure goes well. Lauren initially needs a flexible tube of moist air attached to her trach tube because her surgery is fresh, her trach site and her throat need the extra moisture of the humidifier mist for soothing comfort, but it doesn't have to be on twenty-four/seven. It is most important during the initial healing process and when she sleeps, we are advised. They tell us it's finally okay to pick Lauren up from her bed and hold her.

Initially, I'm apprehensive; I don't want to jostle her or accidentally cause her pain. Plus, I am frightened and intimidated by the trach tube. It is literally her lifeline. It is also a bit disgusting, like a nose that continuously drips mucus, and requires frequent suctioning, which the nurses teach us to do.

Jim and I both are medical novices in that we have never been exposed to or had to handle anything related to surgery or its aftermath. Lovingly and longingly, we agree to learn to do WIT (whatever it takes) in our new role as special needs parents.

Although I am so eager to hold my baby girl in my arms, I am also worried that I may innocently hurt her by bumping or moving that thing sticking out of her neck. As I pick Lauren up, she is a bit floppy because of her Down syndrome and her sedation. I need to be extra careful in supporting her head to make certain that her chubby baby neck doesn't occlude this tube that is critical for her breath and her very life.

After I've mastered picking Lauren up, I have to learn to suction her trach tube. It scares me to death. I have insert a thin, clear tube into the opening and about six inches down her throat, then turn on the suctioning device and suck up the mucus for fifteen seconds. Initially, this needs to be done every thirty minutes, but as time goes on, it becomes less frequent. I am little bit proud of myself: here I am, a woman who could barely stomach putting a tampon in a year ago, and now I am putting a plastic tube down my child's throat so that she can clear her airway. I am determined. I will do what it takes to help my child.

There's good stuff, too. It is miraculous to hold Lauren, to play with her, to cuddle her gently, and to sing and talk to her. We bring in soft toys and stuffed animals for her to see. Because of her chest wound and the fact that babies don't know to restrict their movements, she is sedated daily—and although she is interactive and smiles, it is obvious that she is on drugs. The more she recovers, though, the more the sedation is reduced. I sense that Lauren knows that we are her parents despite living in this sterile environment filled with myriad strange faces and hands bombarding her each day. Her subtle responses fill my heart with joy.

We learn that babies like classical music, so we buy a Fisher-Price child's tape recorder and an array of classical cassettes and play them for Lauren frequently. We ask the staff to put on a long tape for her at her bedtime, when we are not there.

It is difficult for babies, especially babies with Down syndrome, with their low muscle tone, to control their throat muscles and swallow with a trach stuck in their neck. So although I try to give Lauren a mini-bottle, she is not able to eat or drink well enough to sustain herself—which means that we soon get another bit of medical education: how to feed Lauren through a nasogastric (NG) tube.

This delicate and intimidating process takes only about a minute to do but feels like an eternity due to our fear factor. To begin, it requires Lauren to be lying down calmly on her back. Jim holds her head straight while I perform the task. I gingerly pick up the thin, clear plastic tubing to insert into one of Lauren's nostrils. Then I carefully guide and push it in and pray that it goes down straight to her throat and (hopefully) into her stomach. Although this sounds relatively simple to accomplish, it is not. Last step is to check my accuracy by placing a stethoscope on Lauren's stomach and pressing to see if I can hear a whoosh of air. It's a scary and serious process that could be life threatening if not performed correctly. I get to do this—a wimp who can't watch her own blood being drawn. But once again, it is amazing what we learn to do out of love for our precious baby.

There is no choice, really. I love my little girl, and I will learn and do anything to help make her well. As I go through these scary, necessary procedures, I just keep reminding myself of the day that I spent with Pat and Jillian and how they both recovered from similar trauma. I try not to dwell on the sadness of our lost dreams and pray that none of these nasty procedures is hurting Lauren. I am amazed at what I have become capable of in just a few short weeks.

Feeding is a challenge, but the scariest procedure of all so far is the changing of Lauren's trach tube, which we must do every other day for hygiene. It demands careful preparation of all supplies and swift movement: remove the dirty tube, swipe a sterile cleaning solution near the hole in the throat, and then place a fresh, clean trach tube in the hole and tie fresh cloth laces around her neck to hold it on.

I dread this process. It is so frightening to take my daughter's life in my hands. If I screw up and don't get the clean tube in and positioned properly and quickly enough, she could begin to gasp for breath—and if that happens, I know that I will panic. And changing a trach tube is a two-person process, especially for the inexperienced. Even some of the skilled nurses become apprehensive when they have to do this. I am anxious to take Lauren home, but I am also terrified of what it will be like to handle her medical needs alone at home. *How long will Lauren have to live with these medical devices?* I wonder. *How will we manage? Will this level of care always be necessary? Who will be on watch with her when we sleep? How will I ever go back to work?* The scenarios and the questions weigh heavily on me.

I arrive at the hospital today after having missed an entire day with Lauren—yesterday I had to attend to my own medical appointment and to check in at work with my employer about extending my benefits—and I notice that Lauren's trach has not been changed. The cloth strings around her neck are dirty and wet with mucus. *How could they let this happen?* My blood boils a little.

I try to clean up Lauren's neck while waiting for a nurse to help me change the trach and strings. I lift her head and see that the wet, dirty strings have worn a blistering ridge of sores all around the back of her neck. Because of her Down syndrome, her skin is more sensitive than other babies' and needs more care. I am livid.

"Why hasn't anyone kept up with changing my daughter's trach tube and laces?" I demand when a nurse enters the room. "I was only gone one day!"

No one will own up to this mistake. The anger I feel over this mismanagement of my daughter's care, and my simultaneous heartache over the pain that this carelessness has caused her, will become familiar to me as time goes on, although I do not know this yet.

I maintain my composure as I help with the cleanup and trach tube change. Then I retreat to the ladies' room to weep.

There's a fine line between insisting on the best care and becoming a nuisance to the nurses. I know this. Like it or not (and I don't), Lauren is stuck here for some time. Causing tension or being viewed as a "problem parent" might cause resentment and pushback—and I don't want to do anything to jeopardize my daughter's getting the best care possible.

I cannot be here twenty-four/seven to watch and to care for Lauren. So I have to find a way to advocate for her without alienating the people we're relying on to keep her alive and on the road to wellness. "We have to cope as best as we can."

The weeks drag on. Monday through Friday we live with either my parents or Jim's; on weekends, we drive the hour to our house in Phoenixville. It's strange to not be in our home. Family members visit Lauren on Friday evenings, Saturdays, and Sundays, when they're not working. We use those Saturdays to catch up on our mail, bills, lawn, laundry, and so on. We are trying to keep up with our lives with only thirty-six hours a week to do it. It's stressful, but somehow we manage it.

We rarely go out or see friends during these weekends. We are still much too fragile—and exhausted—to make time for socializing. In the peace of our home, we think about our "new normal" and all the issues we will be dealing with when Lauren comes home, including where we'll live.

We know we have to move. Because of Lauren's special needs,

we need to be closer to our families, for support, and it would also be wise to be closer to Philadelphia's city center, with its specialty hospitals and physicians. The local hospital and doctors in our small town are not equipped to handle Lauren's complex medical requirements. I also learn from our new friends Pat and Diane that Lauren will need special therapy and an early-intervention preschool. They live in the same suburban township that I grew up in—a place with a stellar school district and programs for special needs children from birth through school age and beyond. Phoenixville has none of this. The handwriting is on the wall.

Between hospital visits and weekend life maintenance, we begin searching for a new home in the Lafayette Hill area and preparing to sell our home in Phoenixville (let's pile one more demand on our shoulders, shall we?). Thankfully, our home is in above-average condition—we have done some remodeling over the past five years to give it a more contemporary look, and it is one of the best-kept houses in the neighborhood—so we are confident that it will sell.

The challenge will be to find a comparable new home in Lafayette Hill. We can't do a fixer-upper; we need a house that will essentially be in move-in condition. We will be too preoccupied with Lauren's homecoming and her special care to engage in our own version of *Extreme Makeover: Home Edition*. But homes in Lafayette Hill, with its desirable location, command higher prices than comparable homes in Phoenixville. So we need to spend time—time we don't have—evaluating our finances to determine what we can afford. And since I still don't know when, or if, I'll be able to go back to work, this is even more difficult.

This question—whether or not I'll be able to keep my job—looms ominously on our minds. With Lauren's condition, we don't know if we can rely on Jim's small-business health plan to cover her health costs. The medical bills and invoices have begun to come in over the past few weeks, and the numbers we're seeing are frightening. When I lie in bed at night, the questions run through my mind in a loop: *What if I can't return to work? How will we ever obtain good insurance coverage with Lauren's serious preexisting conditions? If we do find a good plan, what will it cost us? Will the insurance pay for overnight care so that we can both sleep without worrying that something might happen to Lauren? How will I perform simple daily tasks like food marketing, banking, shopping, or simply taking a walk if Lauren has these needs?*

And, of course, the most basic question: *Will our lives ever be normal again?*

Unwanted Life Lessons

L et's talk about life lessons. We are learning many of them as our daughter, and we, continue to spend our days confined to this hospital.

They don't teach these lessons in even the finest schools. You won't learn them in birthing classes or while swapping labor and delivery stories with your friends. Even the school of hard knocks would cringe at them. These are the life lessons nobody wants.

Nobody wants them because they inevitably involve grief, pain, trauma, fear, frustration, and anger for you and your family. You can't explain them to friends, coworkers, and extended family, because unless they've been there, they can't understand. And even if they do ask you to tell them about what's going on, most have no idea how to respond or support you. You feel a terrible, lonely sense of wisdom, isolated here in your new world of endless watching, waiting, hoping, and praying.

Crisis dislocates you. You're plucked from your comfortable, carefully cultivated life and dropped into circumstances where you have no information and no control, where you careen between terror, anger, and exhaustion—and are then asked to make rational decisions in spite of it all. It's *The Twilight Zone* come to life. You wonder aloud if you're dreaming. "Is this really happening?" you ask your equally bewildered, battered partner. But he is just as lost as you are.

This is how we feel all the time as our vigil at William Penn Memorial continues. Everything has happened so quickly; Jim and

I live in a perpetual daze. Our goals and dreams are at worst obsolete, at best on hold indefinitely. Strangers control our schedules and our lives, and we face possible financial catastrophe. *How did we get here? Did this really happen to us and our beautiful baby?*

I understand why the doctors and other health-care professionals we're meeting keep themselves emotionally separate from our case. It's sheer self-defense. It's probably the only thing that keeps them sane in the face of random death and tragedy—a stillborn baby, a high school football star who becomes a quadriplegic, that sort of thing. But it's hard not to view their distance as callousness. And there's another side to it: their income flows largely from health insurance companies or government insurance programs. They have to follow protocols that maintain the insurers' financial fitness as well as the patient's physical health.

The days turn into weeks and months. Lauren recovers, heals, and grows stronger. I start to see more of myself in her. She has my hair color and texture, my brown eyes, and my complexion. She reminds me of my youngest sister, Rose, when she was a baby. Rose is ten years younger than me, and I used to love dressing her up in frilly clothes and playing with her. My precious Lauren reminds me of those days, especially now that we are allowed to put baby nightgowns and pajamas on her. Even this small change does much to make things seem less institutional. We bring in more stuffed animals and small toys to hang in her crib.

Each day, my bond with Lauren grows. We're learning to ignore her trach and her NG tubes when we pick her up and cuddle her. When I look at her now, I barely see her many medical accessories; I just see my beautiful daughter.

The wounds from the heart surgery and the tracheotomy are healing well, to the point where Lauren can have a few visitors. Some of our extended family and siblings come to meet her, treading softly in this high-tech baby ICU. They know we are too exhausted by our ordeal to instruct them or explain what's going on, so they don't ask. They simply coo over the newest family member—and pretend that things aren't scary and strange right now, that we aren't in the NICU with a sick infant. We are grateful for their sensitivity—for their willingness to do this for us.

Another stressor is in my sights now. My HMO has been calling me (read: harassing me) about taking Lauren home, and they won't stop. Today, the phone rings again. Against my better judgment, I answer.

My HMO assigned caseworker, Ms. Penny Pincher, has been hounding the hospital and Lauren's attending physicians about when she may be discharged. I suspect that Ms. Pincher and her employer are more concerned with the cost containment of our huge medical expenses than what Lauren's care plan will be once she is home. Our phone conversations have taken a sinister tone now as she tries to make me feel guilty and selfish as a mother who is not anxious to take her new baby home. "Mrs. Barker, aren't you anxious to get your baby home with you and your family? Don't you hate leaving her alone in the hospital each evening? I'm sure that you will be able to find people to help you with her care once you are home."

I counter her pressure tactics with questions and concerns about how we will safely manage our baby's care. She offers little advice nor in-home care and support solutions. Although her spin does indeed make me feel judged, my gut tells me otherwise. I stand my ground.

Bring Lauren home now? It's inconceivable. How could Jim and I cope on our own with a fragile baby and all these medical devices? Even if one of us quit our job to stay home, who would stay awake all night to care for her trach tube so that she doesn't choke to death? We can't afford a nurse's fifty-dollars-per-hour salary out of our own pockets. And day care is clearly out of the question. I can't imagine how we'd ever find a nonprofessional competent enough to be Lauren's nanny. My intuition and logic tell me that this is a fantasy.

I strongly suspect that once we agree to take Lauren home, we are on our own. It is assumed that we will "figure it out." Right. At what cost? Our sanity? Our health? Our jobs? Our home? We desperately want to take our precious baby girl home with us, but we know we lack the training and resources to handle her care by ourselves. Lauren no longer requires NICU-level care, but with her trach and feeding tube, it is not feasible for her to be on a regular children's hospital floor. She needs to be attended to more often than the standard patient/nurse ratio on a regular hospital floor would allow: her trach tube not being cleared quickly could create a life-threatening situation, a liability that our HMO wants to avoid. *But it's fine for Jim and me to care for her at home with no medical training!?* I want to scream into the phone at them.

If you develop a serious health problem, it's likely that, at some point, you will have to do battle with your health insurance company over the care that they will pay for and the services you will be allowed to access. Unfortunately, the quality of the health care you receive often comes down to who fights the longest and hardest—and insurers usually win that war, because they have resources dedicated to determining what care is warranted and what care isn't, while you're busy trying to cope with the emotional drain of being sick and trying to take care of your job and your family. What I find after a lot of back and forth, however, is that if you are persistent and organized, you can get your insurance company to compromise.

The first compromise is this: three months after her birth, in mid-July, Lauren is transferred to a step-down children's hospital. My hope is that this will be a less stressful environment than the NICU, with its twenty-four/seven bright lights, alarms, and constant parade of medical professionals.

The hospital we're sent to is called the Youth Rehabilitation Hospital—or, as most of the patients and staff refer to it, "the Rehab." While it's much closer to our home and in a pleasant suburban setting, the hospital itself is just as drab and depressing as William Penn. The Rehab looks like it was a real hospital at some point but was abandoned for more modern facilities fifty years ago. It's clean enough, but it's obviously very dated.

As we make the arrangements for Lauren's transfer there, the HMO intensifies the pressure on us to solidify near-future plans to take her home. They now ask the hospital social worker, Karen, to be their mouthpiece.

Karen explains that Ms. Pincher and the HMO have offered this step-down unit stay as an olive branch to us—to give us more time to learn and feel more comfortable with Lauren's extraordinary medical care needs. As a mother of young children herself, I know that she sees the intense pain and ambiguity I am experiencing over my fears. She knows that we love Lauren dearly, but we are still so shocked and frightened about her fragility. She recommends that we take this next step because we all agree that the acute NICU is no longer warranted. She is familiar with the Rehab and assures me that it will be less intense emotionally for all of us there.

Thankfully, we have a terrific benefits person at my work who has taken a personal interest in my case; in one conversation, she advises me that I am eligible for extended paid leave—due to my acute emotional state, she says, I can claim that I am totally incapable of performing my job at this time. It's true; there's no way I could do my job right now. So I apply for the disability pay, and my wonderful employer grants it without putting up a fight. Because my work is commission only, I'm making only about half of my usual weekly pay, but any income is welcome at this point.

In our three months at William Penn Memorial, not once did anyone offer Jim or me any sort of counseling or assistance dealing with the incredible stress—not the doctors, not the social workers. Our only help in that department has come from Jim's aunt, who is a psychologist. Doris referred me to a counselor named Katie, and I've met with her on a number of occasions now, but I do not find our sessions helpful. It's good to be able to vent for an hour each week about my situation, but I don't think that someone who hasn't gone through what Jim and I are experiencing—even a professional—can imagine the life-altering trauma that we are experiencing well enough to guide me through it in a meaningful way.

Our short-lived sessions consisted of me sitting rigidly in a chair opposite of Katie, wringing my hands incessantly in my lap as we speak. I am conscious of this odd hand fidgeting, but I know it is a much-needed physical aid to help me extract the very difficult thoughts and words I am struggling to say to her. What I share is intense. I feel guilty for initially rejecting Lauren. I am angry that this happened to us since I was so careful with my health while pregnant. I feel sick about all of the pain that my precious baby has had to endure. I am sad about my smashed dreams and not being able to experience the happiness typical of a new mother. I feel frightened and unqualified about not being able to care for my child with her fragile medical condition. I am terrified of losing all that I have worked so hard for these many years. I yearn for someone to tell me that everything will be okay. That we will get through this fine and that our lives will be normal and happy, albeit changed.

Katie listens intently and asks the appropriate prodding questions, but she doesn't get it. She continuously poses open-ended, canned questions with no guidance nor answers. "Liz, how are you coping with your daughter's unexpected situation?" She cares, but she can't fathom my personal pain. In reality, no one can, unless you've been in my shoes.

And then there's the emotionally draining, hard-nosed business side of it to deal with too—battling with the insurance company for proper care. This has taken quite a toll on me over time.

What I really want is advice on how to effectively deal with my HMO, and Katie isn't much help there. But I suppose she's better than nothing. At least I can vent and dump my feelings on her without guilt because she is a paid professional.

Despite its shabby appearance, we already like the Rehab much better than William Penn. We've met a whole new stable of medical professionals here, and I've found that most of the nursing staff is quite nice, as are the doctors. The atmosphere is much more laid back, which I like.

Several therapists have turned their attention to both Lauren and me. I'm learning how to work with Lauren to build up her muscles, which are weak due to her extended sedation and her Down

syndrome. Meanwhile, speech, physical, and occupational therapists are working with her to help her develop her abilities in those
areas.

Today, I watch speech therapist Andy attempt to teach Lauren
to suck, drink, and eat—something she hasn't done yet. Although
I spend time with her every day, feeding her with a preemie bottle,
she cannot yet ingest enough food to sustain herself. The NG feeding tube is a constant companion.

I really like Andy. With her patience and enthusiasm, it is so evident that she loves working with children. She shows me how to best
position Lauren in a sit-up seat so that her neck and trach are not
occluded and how to patiently hold the bottle at a certain angle for
easy flow. I follow her coaching carefully, and Lauren ingests slowly.
But I can't help secretly wondering and worrying how Lauren man-
ages to breathe from the tube in her throat while simultaneously
drinking liquids. How does she not choke?

So while it's amazing to see Lauren making some progress, I'm
still feeling a lot of stress—and it seems to be playing havoc with my
immune system. I am caught in a nasty cycle of annoying illnesses:
runny nose, stuffy head, fatigue, bleary eyes, and slight fever. The
more worn out I am, the worse I get. I've been in and out of bed with
these flulike symptoms for a couple of months now. I know that this
is happening because I am pushing myself too hard, but I don't feel
like I have much choice in the matter. I ignore my body's warning
signs of fatigue and stress and press on.

The gods smile on us in the form of an eager realtor named Al who
has a young family of his own. He understands our situation completely. Working with him, we find a wonderful new home on our
first round of appointments. It is older than our present home, but
it is well built and has a spacious split-level layout. The abbreviated
staircases that lead up and down to each level seem ideal for small
children. It has a nicely landscaped, fenced yard and is in move-in
condition. And when Jim and I sharpen our pencils, pull out our

calculator, our bills, and our savings statements and crunch the numbers, we find that we can afford this house.

The sellers, a kindly retired couple, learn of our plight with Lauren and make negotiations easy. We sign our agreement of sale on July 15 with a proposed settlement and move-in date of September 15.

On the ride home from the Al's office after signing the papers, I wonder aloud, "Where will we all be by September 15?" The uncertainty of our lives is daily weight on our shoulders. Still, this is a lightbulb moment. I'm realizing what a thick mental fog we've been in. *We need to get our lives back on track,* I think. *And this house is the first step in that direction.*

But the list of things we need to do next is overwhelming. I need a plan for returning to my job so that I can keep our health insurance plan. We need to get a commitment and a care plan from our damned HMO to cover care for Lauren at home. We need a new pediatrician. And we need to see about getting Lauren into the special needs preschool therapy program that Pat's and Diane's girls attend—a program that will provide Lauren with ongoing physical, speech, and occupational therapy services.

The "infant program" (for children up to age three) we want to place Lauren in requires that a parent or caregiver be onsite and sometimes participate in therapy as the first step of a lifelong plan for their special needs child, but it's funded by the state and the federal government, so it's blessedly free. The program is called the Arc Alliance. The laws that have made this possible state that special needs children, from birth through age eighteen, are entitled to education and training that will enable them to become productive citizens. I hope whoever wrote that legislation receives a special spot in heaven.

I meet with Alice, the director of the Rehab, to discuss our HMO's discharge plan for Lauren. Naïvely, I don't contact an attorney or other advocate to accompany me to the meeting.

It's clear that Alice has an agenda courtesy of the HMO: discharge Lauren to our home, for us to care for solely on our own. But by the end of the meeting, she is moved enough by our love for Lauren and our fears for her health to promise to try to sway the HMO into providing some caregiver service to us at home.

At the onset of the meeting, Alice states that the agenda is about getting Lauren home with us as soon as possible. She doesn't know us personally at all. She soon will, though, as I challenge her with the same specific questions that I posed to Ms. Pincher back at the hospital—"Who will watch over Lauren at night while we sleep? Who will be there to ensure that she does not choke or suffocate to death with her trach through the night?" This, of course, assumes that I don't go back to work and that I am allowed to continue my disability and, with it, our valuable health insurance plan. After we have these friendly debates, Alice realizes that we love our daughter and we want the best care for her. She understands the obvious, that one of us has to go to work and that the caregiver at home, me, can't be up twenty-four/seven or run on little sleep and still offer competent care. She sees that we don't want to shirk our responsibilities to our child and that we are rightfully fearful of inadvertently harming her. We simply want some nighttime care until the trach is removed.

After meeting with Alice, I begin to ask the nurses about what other parents like us have done after release. It turns out that there haven't been many parents like us.

I befriend one other mother whose baby has a feeding tube and whose insurance company is going to pay for in-home nursing care to help her and her husband cope—but she doesn't have an HMO. And even Diane and Pat cannot guide me: they both were on maternity leave by the time their daughters were healed from surgery and sent home, and neither of their girls were encumbered with a feeding tube and a trach, which meant they had the option of finding day cares for their babies.

I speak with another young mother whose child has a breathing disorder. They sent her baby home with her from the regular hospital, but her baby's nighttime needs were too much for her and her husband to manage while holding down jobs and caring for their other children. The baby is now in the Rehab, where he will stay until he grows well enough to need less care.

Though it's better than William Penn, the Rehab is lonely and depressing. I have found few other parents to talk to about coping strategies—many of the babies here have parents that are teenaged, incompetent, or uncaring (or all three). The other day, I met a thirteen-year-old mother of twins whose mother, the twins' grandmother, is my age! And there are multiple babies here who, born sick, have been abandoned by their mothers. Hearing this, I am incredulous. *How can you drop off your baby for repair like an old pair of shoes and never come back for them?* The thought makes me sick.

One baby boy's story twists my gut in knots. He was born in a toilet to a teenager who tried to flush him away. He was half drowned and brain damaged when someone in the bathroom heard the ruckus and saved his life—if you can call it that. Harold is now twelve months old and is still the size of an infant. He is mentally retarded and blind, and has both a trach and a feeding tube. He does not crawl or climb. He is kept in a dark corner of the unit and never has visitors. His only interaction with people comes when the nurses feed or change him. I would walk over to his crib to see him, but he was profoundly retarded and I don't know if he sensed that I was there. He, too, had a trach and a feeding tube, so I didn't dare to touch him. And, sadly, I was too emotionally distraught with our own situation to become emotionally involved with his.

Two weeks ago, one of the nurses at the Rehab told me that Harold was being transferred to a different facility. Today, I overhear a conversation between two of the nurses here.

"Did you hear about Harold?" one asks.

"No," the other says. "What happened?"

"He died two days ago," the first nurse says. "The staff at the ill-trained nursing home he got transferred to neglected his trach and he choked to death."

The other nurse clucks sympathetically. "That's terrible."

I, meanwhile, burst into tears. I weep not just for Harold but also out of the fear that this could happen to Lauren. The thought is devastating.

Surprisingly enough, however, what happens to Harold is a sort of wake-up call for both the Rehab's staff and our HMO. Between that tragic incident and Alice's feedback, our HMO proposes doing away with Lauren's nasal feeding tube and instead replacing it with a gastrointestinal tube—a flexible tube that provides a direct line to the stomach and can be capped with a clip. This will allow us to feed her more easily as we continue to coax her to drink and eat by mouth. It's supposed be safer, too: they tell us it will eliminate the risk of her aspirating food into her lungs, which is always a possibility with the NG tube. But it will require another surgery.

It's late August now; four months have passed since Lauren's birth. We are all weary of the hospital environment and dealing with the circus of strangers barking orders and mandates. Yet through all the pokes, prods, therapies, and such, Lauren is a sweet baby. She never cries. She smiles and coos and blows raspberries at us with her pursed baby lips. I dress her daily in her little baby girl clothes—an attempt to make our situation seem somewhat normal—and I read to her and sing to her along with her little tape recorder and tapes. Sometimes we even get to disconnect her from the moist air tube attached to her trach and take her outside in a stroller.

Today, I take Lauren outside for one of our walks. I sit down on a bench for a moment, and sitting there, my baby in a stroller next to me, I marvel at how overjoyed I am to be doing something as simple as sitting peacefully with fresh air, sunshine, and nature sounds. It is a reprieve from the air-conditioned, zero-privacy, institutional setting I've become all too used to. I dream about us being free of this and of Lauren's physical constraints. I allow myself to relive some of my lost dreams of having a baby to take home and to do fun "Mommy and me" things with: walks, visits with friends, shopping.

After a few moments of this fantasy, reality intrudes, and I remember: the entire summer is gone, and with it the dreams Jim and I had of playing with our baby at the beach or taking her on weekend trips. *But there is some nice fall weather to be had,* I remind myself, *and we get to share it with our daughter.* It feels like it's time to begin to develop some new dreams—dreams based on this reality—and see if we can still find happiness.

Today is the day that Lauren will have the surgery to insert the gastrointestinal tube. We're back at William Penn Memorial for this, because the Rehab is not equipped for such procedures. We have not been looking forward to this return to the Badlands. We have been spoiled by the Rehab's suburban setting. But after a recovery period of about a week, Lauren should finally be able come home—and miracle of miracles, the HMO has agreed to pay for in-home nursing care with a qualified registered nurse. The nurse's shift will begin at 8:00 p.m. and end at 8:00 a.m. each day, giving Jim and me a chance to sleep, and also providing me with a skilled partner for changing the trach tube. Knowing that we will have this help and plan eases many of my fears.

Lauren's surgery has just started, and we are sitting in the waiting room and chatting with other families enduring their own children's illnesses or surgeries. But it's hard to carry a conversation: we are anxious. Lauren is still weak from her sedations, surgeries, and confinement, and her Down syndrome makes her vulnerable to begin with. Any medical procedure is harder for her than most other babies her age.

One father's heartbreaking story catches my attention, however.

"My wife and I have two other small children at home," he's telling Jim, "so my wife can't always come to the hospital with me. Most of the time, it's just me here."

"That must be really hard," Jim says. "Being here by yourself."

The man nods. "The worst part is, I got fired a couple of weeks ago for missing so much time from work to be with my kid. So not only have we lost our sole income, but we may lose our health insurance." He buries his head in his hands.

I lay my hand on his shoulder. "That's terrible," I say. "I'm so sorry."

Listening to his story, I feel sick. Sometimes you just need a helping hand to avoid ruin. Shouldn't everyone get at least that? I am so grateful that my own employer is being so supportive throughout this ordeal.

Lauren's procedure went flawlessly, and her new gastrointestinal tube isn't so bad—it's hidden under her clothing. I am upset that she had to endure another surgery, but she seems fine—she was all smiles when we came to see her afterward. She is such a trooper. She doesn't appear traumatized at all. And now we are one step closer to leaving this place: Lauren's homecoming day will be September 8.

Unfortunately, that is just one week from our moving day. Because we haven't had enough stress thus far, we decided to pile on a little more. Jim and I will be presiding over the closing of two escrows in one day, moving, unpacking, and settling in while simultaneously caring for an infant with special needs. We're either superhuman or crazy.

The upside is that our Phoenixville house has sold already, and for our full asking price. Because we were hardly ever there in these past few months, it was always neat as a pin, and Al could show it at any time. Today, we're working on packing stuff up.

I've never been a hoarder, so the packing itself has been relatively easy. And our wonderful brothers and sisters have come to help over the past couple of weekends, streamlining the process even more. But as we box up our things, my eyes begin to well up with tears—not because I am attached to this house, but because I recall how joyous it was when we moved in, and all of our grand dreams for not only the house but our lives. I remember how several close friends—also young married couples—helped us move in and then celebrated with us afterward. Those were great times—all us young, ambitious couples just starting out, full of high hopes and expectations. The people we were then appear distant now.

Life seems like a spinning top. When will we slow down? What lies ahead? Only time will tell. For now, we at least are maintaining our balance.

Homecoming

Finally, five months after her birth, Lauren is coming home. It's odd; we simply missed spring and summer. It's as if they didn't happen. But we're ready to be free of institutions and authorities. The fog has lifted somewhat. We have mapped out our revised life plan and are moving forward with it. Lauren's original surgical wounds are healed, and she seems to have no psychological wounds from the past few months. She is a happy, pleasant baby. We have learned how to feed her with her new gastrostomy tube (G-tube), and we are more comfortable with her trach care now. We have also learned CPR (which we hope we never have to use). And we have a new home that will keep us closer to our family and our new friends.

We've enrolled Lauren in the special needs infant program at the Arc Alliance. When we went there to fill out the application, we met a child advocate named Patty, who is a godsend. I wish I'd met her months ago. She wrestled with our HMO on our behalf (and she admitted that it was quite a battle) to get them to agree to our home care arrangement on a long-term basis, not just for the three weeks. Patty knew exactly what our health concerns were. She made the HMO understand their responsibilities for Lauren's safety and what their liabilities would be if something happened to her due to inadequate care from their skimping. Ironically, it would likely have been far less expensive for the HMO if they had simply agreed to pay for at-home care months ago. It would also have saved our family, and me especially, from the extreme stress that has come with months spent at hospitals. But thanks to Patty, our HMO is now providing us with a nighttime home nurse *and* an RN who accompanies me to Lauren's doctor appointments.

Otherwise, however, we're going to be on our own. Once we bring Lauren home, if I want to venture out—to shop, to go to the doctor, to visit a hair salon, whatever—I will need to wait until Jim gets home. Both our sets of parents are still working, and at any rate they are neither trained nor comfortable with the trach and G-tubes.

But that will come later. For now, we're just excited that Lauren is being released today (I feel like calling it "emancipation day"). Jim and I are all dressed up, and we've brought our camera with us to document the occasion. I got Lauren a homecoming outfit: a beautiful smocked-top white dress dotted with tiny pink roses, with cute puffy short sleeves and a full skirt. She looks so pretty in it. Since she's had a full head of hair since the day she was born, I brought a little pink bow for her hair as well. All dressed up like this, she looks so much like me when I was a baby.

Despite the trauma she has been through, Lauren continues to be a pleasant baby who rarely cries. She is truly a happy child, and we have formed an unbreakable bond despite (or perhaps because of) the circumstances. Her patience and acceptance of all that she has experienced are a huge life lesson to me. As I sit here holding her, getting ready to bring her home, I know that I have never felt a love like this. Perhaps my love for her is especially poignant because of what we have been through together.

God, please let our love and our lifetimes together be long and happy, I pray silently.

We've earned that much, haven't we?

We take pictures and say our good-byes to the nursing staff at William Penn, then strap Lauren into her car seat. The smile never leaves her face. I am certain that she senses that this is a big day. We are finally doing something that's normal for new parents: taking our baby for a ride in our car.

Lauren's trach tube is a problem. When she's sitting up, we

always have to watch her and position her so that her chin and neck don't occlude the tube opening. The trach has a small, clear piece of tubing on it that serves as a soft extension that's supposed to prevent her chubby baby chin from covering her breathing hole, but sometimes it slips off. We've noticed that Lauren is smart enough to lift her chin to clear the trach when this happens—but that only makes us feel marginally better about it. It's a situation that has us on guard during every waking moment; we can never truly relax.

Today Jim is driving, so I can sit in the backseat with Lauren and make sure her trach stays clear—but I worry about being in the car alone with her. If her tube were to pop off, would I be able to pull over fast enough to help her? In the past few weeks, in preparation for her coming home, I've altered my driving habits: I always drive in the right lane, so I can pull over more easily, and I've started to avoid treacherous, busy roads like the Schuylkill Expressway. I feel a little paranoid having to change my habits, but driving more conservatively makes me feel better.

When we pull into our driveway, Jim and I take turns photographing each other carrying Lauren into our home. It's a beautiful, sunny day. Our families will arrive this evening for dinner and to celebrate Lauren's homecoming. We even have a champagne toast ready. I feel hopeful.

Jim snaps one last photo and we head inside to show Lauren her new home (at least for the next week) and her nursery. We can hardly believe that this is finally happening. We take lots of photos of her in her new room and with her stuffed animals and toys; I cover up her trach with her dress collar. I can't help but cry—but they're tears of happiness. The fact that the nursery is full of special equipment for Lauren's trach and G-tube care does not dampen my joy.

We feed Lauren her lunch via her G-tube and put her down for a nap in her cozy new pajamas so she'll be awake when our families come over later tonight. It's such simple thrill to finally use our changing table. Now that our girl is home, even simple things are a tremendous joy and relief.

Dinner is warm and wonderful. We make many toasts. Both of Lauren's grandmothers hold her and become teary eyed. Lauren loves being passed around as the guest of honor. Everyone marvels that she has already outgrown her cradle; she's sleeping in her regular crib in her nursery. Her overnight nurse will be able to relax comfortably in the nursery's rocker.

As we're cleaning up after dinner, our home care nurse arrives.

We will have a short list of three or four of these nurses, whom the nursing agency will schedule and rotate as their availability and schedules allow. We introduce Ann to our family and to Lauren and offer her some leftovers and cake. She tells us about her many years of nursing. She talks lovingly about caring for her aged parents as their health declined, an experience that brought her into home care. She has both trach and G-tube know-how with children and enjoys night work more than day shifts. Not only is she well qualified for Lauren's care, but she fits in like an extended family member.

As the night winds to an end, our families say their good-byes, and Jim and I get ready to go to bed. Before I turn in, I go into Lauren's nursery and gently kiss her. I look down at her, sleeping there in her own peaceful bed where she belongs, and I feel at peace. For the first time in her life, she won't spend the night in a noisy hospital.

And for the first time in months, Jim and I both fall asleep easily and sleep soundly. We're at ease knowing that our baby is home and that she is under a watchful eye this night.

We awake at 7:00 a.m. and tiptoe over to Lauren's room. Ann is awake in the rocker, but Lauren is asleep.

"How did it go?" I whisper.

"Great," Ann whispers back. "She didn't wake up once, except for her 4:00 a.m. feeding."

Jim and I exchange looks of relief. This is going to work.

We all have coffee and then Ann and I prepare Lauren for her day.

I am relieved that we don't have to change her trach today, since it only has to be done every three days now.

"What has it been like these past five months?" Ann asks as we get Lauren changed and dressed. "It must have been so difficult, having her in the hospital all this time."

I tell her about everything we've been through, and she listens with a sympathetic face. She seems genuinely caring. I hope that the rest of the nurses are just as nice. I have determined that I will no longer tolerate people who are rude or condescending—not when they're around my daughter, anyway. I have taken enough attitude from health-care and insurance professionals to last me for the rest of my life.

"How do you stay awake through the night?" I ask. I'm sure I couldn't do it.

"I bring a reading light for my books," she explains. "Although it is hard to read all night long. Actually, with your permission, I'd love to bring a small, portable TV with me next time. It really helps to pass the time."

"I think that would be fine," I say. "And you don't have to be in the nursery the whole time, either; you can sit in the spare bedroom next to Lauren's room, if you like." The spare room is fully furnished, so Ann will be more comfortable there, but still so close to Lauren's room that she'll be able to hear her if she stirs. After we move, Lauren's bedroom will be more spacious and there will also be a spare bedroom right next to it for her nurse.

The next few days pass quickly and pleasantly. Although I am housebound with Lauren, there is much to do. I relish it. I have much to catch up with from my life, and it's marvelously peaceful not to make the daily commute to a hospital. Our stress, while not gone, is diminished. While Lauren naps, I call friends, family, and coworkers and make appointments for her doctors, therapists, and educational programs. I also check in with my office. Lauren is now enrolled in the infant program at the Arc Alliance, and I am looking forward to this new adventure—to meeting professionals who will help Lauren grow strong both mentally and physically. There is an active parent support group there, too. I can't wait to talk with and learn from these parents who have children with similar special needs.

Pat and Diane have also told me about a local chapter of the Down Syndrome (DS) Interest Group for our county, which they both belong to, and which they have encouraged me to join. The best part is, it meets every month at our local library in Lafayette Hill, just five minutes from our new home. Jim and I are looking forward to meeting other parents of children with DS there. We are anxious to meet people who can relate to and understand our fears and concerns about our children's future. We have so many questions!

Gradually, more and more bits of normal life—our new normal life—are coming back into focus.

We're moving in two days, and Sue, who will be one of our regular nurses, too, has just arrived. She volunteers some background information without my even having to ask.

"I've been nursing for a long, long time," she says. "But of all the jobs I've had, doing in-home care for special needs children and babies is what I love most."

She seems bright and experienced. She and Ann chat about their professional lives, and they decide to exchange phone numbers in case they have questions about Lauren's care or need to follow up. I love the harmony.

Sue is here to accompany me on my long drive over to the Arc's infant program. These federally funded programs are set up for each county. Because we are moving to Lafayette Hill, which is in Montgomery County, we are bound to the program that is in our new county. It's about forty minutes from our old house but will only be about ten minutes from our new house.

"Before we go, as long as I'm here, why don't we change Lauren's trach?" Sue asks.

I gulp and nod. "Okay."

This still makes me terribly nervous. We must follow a specific sequence of steps quickly and efficiently: remove the old tube; clean the area; put a new, sterile tube into her neck hole; put the straps on the trach and tie it in place; and then apply foam adhesive padding to the strings so they won't chafe and burn Lauren's neck. It's a two-person job that requires synchronization, especially in the final stage, when one person holds the trach in place while the other ties on the strings and adds the padding. Because they have such soft skin and their necks and cheeks are usually chubby, it's sensitive work doing this on a baby. Oh, and did I mention that we also need to keep Lauren lying down and still as we do this? No problem, right?

Thankfully, Lauren is pleasant and cooperative. She lies there, docile, as Sue and I put a wide Band-Aid on her clavicle (to guard against chafing) and fit the clear tube extender onto her trach. Jim had the smart idea of buying a long length of clear plastic tubing, cutting it in two-inch pieces, and using that to extend Lauren's trach instead of the hard plastic extension piece the hospital gave us, which always abrades her skin. We're getting more comfortable with discarding advice that doesn't work and finding our own solutions.

I exhale as we finish our nerve-racking task. *We did it!* I smile at Sue. I'm grateful to have someone so competent here to help me.

We pack up the car and venture out. With Sue here to keep an eye on Lauren, I'm finally able to enjoy being out and about with my baby. Again, I am relishing simple pleasures. This week at home with Lauren has been a breath of fresh air. I feel like I've been paroled.

We arrive at the Arc program's offices—housed in a former elementary school—and as we head toward the administrative offices, we pass several little classrooms full of toys, stimulating decorations, and therapy equipment. It is all colorful and friendly and designed for babies and toddlers.

The program director, Jean Todd, and a social worker named Roz, greet us as we enter the administrative office. Both women are warm and welcoming. They explain the program, its educational goals, and how a learning and therapy plan, called an individual program plan, or IPP, will be designed for Lauren's personal needs.

"You'll sit in on most of Lauren's therapy sessions and learn how to do some follow-up exercises at home with her to strengthen her muscles," Jean says. "The Down syndrome makes them weak to begin with, and her long stay in the hospital made them even weaker. So we want to work with her as much as possible to build them back up."

"You are also entitled to a 'respite plan,' " Roz continues. "It's funded by the government, and it offers you a few hours of babysitting each month, done by carefully screened, trained, and mature sitters who have experience with special needs children."

Oh my gosh. Jim and I will actually get to have a date night once in a while! It seems like eons since that's happened. It's good to know that my years of tax payments are going to good use.

Roz takes us to the classrooms. We are scheduled to meet each of Lauren's new team of teachers and therapists. Her main teacher will be Barbara, who will act as the team's point person.

"Welcome," Barbara says, smiling, as we enter the room. She has a kind face and seems patient and experienced. We chat for a few minutes, and she tells me that her own children are grown and she is awaiting grandchildren.

First we meet Lauren's physical therapist, Wendy, a young, single mom who adopted a special needs child of her own. Wendy will address strengthening Lauren's weak muscles and encourage her mobility, all compromised by Down syndrome. Finally, we are enthusiastically greeted by Lauren's speech therapist, Lisa, a dedicated young woman.

I am in awe. It is wonderful to be in this place, meeting these lovely, caring people who are obviously so dedicated to helping special needs children. It's like a toddler heaven—it's filled with toys, books, tricycles, and therapeutic gym equipment. And there's even a parent lounge, which resembles someone's casual den, with a sofa and comfy chairs and TV set—plus toys and books for children, and a high chair and baby seating as well as a toddler table and chairs.

A woman rises from her chair as we enter the lounge.

"Hi," she says, and offers her hand. "I'm Diane Jaroma, the president of the parent group for the program—and this is Connie and

Kate," she gestures to the two women who have walked over to us, "two of the other moms with children here."

"I'm Liz," I say. "So nice to meet you. This lounge is incredible."

Diane smiles. "It's great, isn't it? We set it up ourselves. The parent group is a support and network resource for all parents. We felt like this lounge would be a relaxing place to meet and socialize with other parents. And it also gives siblings of the Arc Alliance kids a place to play while they wait.

I begin to feel something I have not felt since we learned of Lauren's condition: deep gratitude. I would not have wished for what happened to my little girl, but here at this place, I'm being introduced to a warm, welcoming, loving, courageous group of people I would never have come to know otherwise. Fate may have irrevocably changed our life plans, but it has also brought us here.

HMO Stands for "Hand Money Over"

After our upbeat morning, Lauren, Sue, and I head over to a nearby diner. During our pleasant lunch, Sue shows that she is adept at feeding Lauren through her G-tube while simultaneously giving her formula orally. This is done so that Lauren will learn to associate food passing through her mouth with feeling full.

After our meal, we go on to see our new pediatrician.

We have never met Dr. Fossett before—we have only spoken briefly over the phone. He seemed a bit distant and standoffish after I explained Lauren's condition and the reason for my call, but Pat recommended him, so I feel like he must be a good pediatrician. Our phone conversation set off my radar intuition—*something's not quite right here*—but I'm trying to keep an open mind.

The office is in a big old country home that sits in its own old courtyard. It's a very pleasant setting and close to our home. I am optimistic that this will be a good fit for us as we walk in. But the ensuing cold, terse appointment and conversation end my optimism.

Dr. Fossett greets us in a cool manner without even a warm handshake. He has received Lauren's extensive medical file in advance of our visit. He doesn't seem particularly welcoming or enthused about having her as a new patient. His remarks and inquiries about her long hospitalization and time in the Rehab are stinging to me. "Mrs. Barker, five months from birth is a long time for your daughter to have been in medical care. Why is it that you did not see fit to have her home with you prior to this? Her medical bills must have been extraordinary."

I am stunned by his lack of empathy and the fact that he is thinking of dollars and cents over her care. Because the long-running battle wounds with my HMO are still raw, I choke back my tears and emotions and meekly reply, "My husband and I were fearful of Lauren's extensive medical needs, and we did not feel capable of caring for her alone in our home without professional help, especially through the night."

He shoots back a look at me that tells me he is questioning my judgment and my love for my child. He proceeds to examine Lauren swiftly and cursorily. He asks Sue a few of the more technical medical questions about Lauren's condition, and then asks Sue to wait outside with Lauren while we talk. I later understand that he asks Sue to go outside to the waiting area with Lauren because he does not want her to witness what he is about to say to me.

Dr. Fossett then begins to school me in the number one rule in the land of the HMO: *it's all about the money.* Perhaps I'm naïve, but even as a financial professional, I didn't really think in such blatant terms. "Mrs. Barker, let me explain to you how your HMO insurance plan works. HMOs are ideal for healthy patients, who don't require cumbersome and mandatory referrals to specialists. As a participating HMO doctor, it is in the best interest of my practice to *not* refer my patients out to specialists or to have them admitted to a hospital. The more that I have to do these things, the more the HMO will penalize my practice financially."

I find this conversation about the money aspect of health care to be shocking. I think to myself, *So this is why I had such a struggle with the HMO these past months—it's all about the money.*

He goes on to elaborate. "Conversely, my practice will receive incentives and bonus points if I have fewer than the average number of referrals to specialists and hospital admissions." The HMO system uses its primary doctors as its first line of defense for cost-cutting measures. They are actually compensated for discouraging referrals outside of their primary care. Because Lauren still has complex medical issues and will require numerous visits to specialists for her heart, her trach, and her G-tube, having her as his patient will be a financial drain on his practice, he explains.

I'm nauseated by this horrible conversation. Am I supposed to feel sorry for this doctor and his bottom line? I am not a welfare or Medicaid patient, or someone who has never been a productive wage earner. I have been working relentlessly since I was sixteen, and paying hefty taxes and medical insurance premiums all along the way. Lauren's condition is a genetic fluke—it's not like I did something that caused her to have Down syndrome. *How dare this man treat me so disrespectfully?* I think, enraged. *What's the point of paying expensive insurance premiums if the medical profession doesn't want to be bothered with you when you get sick? Isn't that what insurance is for?* All those years when I was fit and healthy and didn't use my coverage, my premiums went to help offset the costs for some other person with medical bills like the ones we have now. *It's my turn now,* I think. *The system owes me.*

Anger pushes blood into my face, but I don't give Dr. Fossett the satisfaction of screaming, though I would like to. He drones on and on, and when he finally shuts up, I ask him if he has the right to refuse us as patients.

"No, I cannot prohibit you from joining this practice," he snaps.

Clearly, I'd be insane to want him as our doctor now! But I can't let his greed and arrogance go unanswered, so I decide to put a little fear into him. Getting up, I say, "Thank you. I'll be in touch after I have called the HMO and my attorney to discuss the matter."

He is aghast. Good. I would have preferred that he had just lied to me and said that he had too many patients, or that Lauren's medical needs were too complex for his small practice. But as I walk out, I realize that he has given me something valuable: a glimpse into the dark side of both the health-care and insurance industries—the belly of the beast, so to speak. I won't forget it.

I pass by the front desk and refuse to hand them the co-pay. Let the HMO or him sue me. Driving away, I am so angry that I cannot even speak to Sue, who is looking at me with concern. Finally, I pull over into a large, empty church parking lot and—after a quick glance back at Lauren, who is asleep—I burst into tears and tell Sue the whole story.

"I've heard of this happening before," she says. She suggests that I follow through on my threats to the doctor: call the HMO and an attorney and ask for advice. I am so drained by this horrible encounter that I can hardly drive. What started out as a dreamy morning at the Arc has turned into a nightmare. And though I don't know it, this is only the beginning: there will be many more unpleasant encounters with our HMO and the world of health care before our journey ends. The battle that began while Lauren was hospitalized rages on; and now it has morphed into a new beast.

We're busy making last-minute preparations for moving to our new home, but I take a break to call our case manager at our HMO and describe yesterday's conversation with Dr. Fossett. While she is shocked at the conversation and the manner in which it was conducted, she admits that that is indeed how the HMO compensation system works.

"He shouldn't have spoken to you that way," she says. "But nothing he said is untrue."

"I intend to write a letter of complaint to your office, the doctor's office, and to the insurance commissioner's office in Harrisburg," I say, disgusted. "This is not okay."

"I understand why you're so upset," she says carefully. "And don't worry—I'll call Dr. Fossett to discuss this with him and to ask him to accept Lauren as a patient."

I don't want him as Lauren's doctor now, but I don't tell her that—instead, I tell her to go ahead and call him. *Why not let her bother and upset him as he did me?* I think. Is that vindictive? I don't care. I am sick of being a victim.

After hanging up with our case manager, I call an attorney I know, though his area of expertise is not medical law. He gives me a pep talk, suggests that I follow my gut in dealing with these people, and tells me to make my demands for fairness loud and clear. I thank him, but I hang up feeling disappointed. What I need most is guidance, not encouragement. But I know no one who understands what we are going through.

I am a fairly intelligent person, but navigating the health-care and insurance systems is mind boggling. For one thing, my mind is not clear: I am suffering from fatigue and stress, and have been for five months. I'm not objective about any of this. But I'm so overwhelmed that I can't see that I am not strong, either physically or mentally, due to my exhaustion. I need a health-care advocate to guide me through this foreign land. But, of course, that's certainly not a benefit any insurance company will offer. So I'm being left to muddle through this as best I can.

I call my only professional lifeline: Patty, the advocate at the Arc. I tell her about the incident with Dr. Fossett and explain that I need to find a good pediatrician for Lauren as soon as possible. She promises to contact Roz to get some referrals from other Arc parents.

Then there's no more time for doctors and insurance companies—it's time to get ready for our move. With Lauren in her musical swing or her bouncy seat, I can be on the portable phone and in her view. She can see and hear me chatting as I call people who will be involved in the move, and I can play with her; it is good stimulus for her.

We sit out on our deck for the last time on this nice September day to have our lunch and enjoy the sunshine, and then I put Lauren down for her long afternoon nap. As soon as she's asleep, I scurry to finish all the last-minute packing tasks: clearing out the refrigerator, the medicine cabinet, my toiletries and makeup, and preparing a day's worth of formula, diapers, and medical supplies for the nurse, who will have Lauren at Jim's parents' house all day while we move everything. I feel overwhelmed by the magnitude of my task; there's not enough time for everything. But I forge ahead. *What other choice do I have?*

Lauren wakes up from her nap cheerful, and I am more than ready to sit and play with her. After I give her some fluids via her G-tube, we settle in with some picture books. Then I do some baby exercises with her to strengthen her weak muscle tone. Then it's into her stroller for a walk up and down our long driveway (I'm still not comfortable going out without the safety of her trach suction equipment nearby).

Lauren is obviously happy. She clearly understands the difference between being in the hospital and being home with us; it shows in her smiling face and her joy in our interactions. We both have far more energy now than when we did when we were cooped up in the sterile hospital. But I can't help thinking about all those months of pain and stress—how much time we lost. I can't help but be angry that our stubborn HMO kept us at those institutions for far longer than necessary because they did not want to pay for in-home care. We spent five months at the mercy of the HMO system. *What a waste.*

I force myself to dismiss these negative thoughts. Instead, I hug and cuddle my perpetually happy daughter. *We're here now, together. That's enough.*

We get a late start the next morning and have to scramble to make up the time. After we leave the house, I go to my in-laws' home to meet Nancy, the nurse who will be looking after Lauren for the day while we are moving in.

She seems very nice and tells me about her family and her young girls; after our conversation, I feel better about leaving Lauren in her care for the day. The plan is for me to come back and pick up Lauren at the end of the day, once we are settled in and the new nursery is ready. Setting up her room is our first priority; we have rented an extra truck that Jim and our fathers will load and unload with her items only.

Somehow, everything goes according to plan. We make it through the Phoenixville settlement and wish the young couple buying our house much luck.

"Thanks so much," the young woman says. "We love this house— we can't wait to live here!" They are first-time buyers who haven't been married very long, and they are full of energy and excitement.

I manage a smile in response. I am glad for them, but seeing their youthful happiness, I also feel a bit wistful. *Jim and I were just like them when we moved into this house,* I think. *And now look at us.*

We wish the young couple well, and for the last time, we back out of our driveway on West Evergreen Drive. We are moving on—and hopefully forward.

The settlement for our new house on Thornhill Drive also goes smoothly. The retired couple from whom we're buying the house surprises us with a gift for Lauren: a stuffed animal. It is amazing how a baby, especially a baby with special needs, can bring out such tenderness in people.

We decide to set Lauren up in the third bedroom temporarily so that we can convert her intended bedroom into a nice nursery. We need to clean it up and get new carpeting in place, and because we've been told that Lauren should have extra stimulation, I also want to paint it a bright, primary color theme. But for now, Lauren and her night nurses simply need a place to sleep and to sit peacefully.

When we go to pick Lauren up, Nancy is all smiles.

"Today went very well," she says. "Lauren is such a pleasant baby! I loved spending time with her."

"Would you be interested in joining the team of nurses we have for Lauren's night care?" I ask hopefully. She is so kind; I would love to have her around.

"I can't do night shift, unfortunately," she says regretfully. "It would be too hard with my little ones' schedules. But if you ever need a daytime nurse, I would be happy to help!"

I'm disappointed, but I understand, of course. She has her own family to tend to. And it's nice to know that there's someone we can trust with Lauren if we ever do need help during the day. "I will definitely keep that in mind," I tell her.

She helps me pack up, and we both go home.

Thornhill Drive is a hive of activity when Lauren and I arrive. My mother is there, and she offers to watch and play with Lauren as I go back to unpacking and organizing. By the end of the day, thanks to our helpers—our brothers and fathers have been assisting with unpacking boxes and reassembling furniture all day—we have accomplished quite a bit. Lauren's crib is made up, our bed is made up, the refrigerator is stocked, and our bathroom and toiletries are set up. We have pizza delivered for dinner, and Jim has planned ahead with a cooler full of ice-cold beer to reward everyone. We also make a champagne toast to Lauren's second homecoming. It is a very happy day.

Everyone heads home about the time that Ann shows up for her shift.

"I love this new place," she enthuses when she arrives. "And it's so close to me!" She lives about a ten-minute drive away.

After tucking Lauren in for the night, Jim and I go to bed far earlier than usual. Somehow, we've gotten through the day. No disasters. No surprises. After five grueling months of uncertainty, fear, and lack of control, we have our daughter here with us, and our move has come off on time, without a hitch. We finally feel like we have our lives back. We are sure that this is the first of many wonderful, happy days ahead. For the first time in what feels like centuries, we are at peace. We pass out quickly when we climb into bed, as much from relief as from exhaustion.

Just Breathe

It's great to be in our new town. Because I grew up here, everything is familiar and reassuring. Our families and many friends are closer. Work is about the same distance away. It's nothing but positive.

We have some short-term goals. We want to settle into the new house; get acquainted with the Arc special needs program; get Lauren weaned off of her trach and her feeding tube so that she can be eligible for day care and so that I can go back to work; and find a good local pediatrician. It's quite a list.

One of the milestones we're eager to reach is to have Lauren formally christened at our church. I want a nice church christening with a fancy, frilly dress, lots of pictures, and a party afterward. After six long months, everyone is anxious to meet her.

We chose Lauren's godparents a long time ago: Jim's younger brother, Jeff, and my good high school friend, Debby. Jeff is a natural choice: he's one year younger than Jim and is married, with his own toddler son and an established career. The godmother decision was more difficult, however. I have three sisters, but they are twenty-four, twenty-three, and nineteen years old, respectively, and I feel that the role of godmother to Lauren, though it is not a legal custodial role, requires someone older and more seasoned. Debby has been a tremendous asset these past five months—not only visiting with Lauren and me but communicating with all our friends about what's going on with us. I know I can count on her.

I feel even better about my choice when Debby shows me the gorgeous long dress with a sheer, matching overcoat and a cute bonnet she bought for Lauren's christening. Jim's mom has bought Lauren a gold bracelet to wear, and his Aunt Doris has bought her a pair of fine leather shoes. We are all set with our date and our plans. We just need one other wish fulfilled before the big day: to have her trach removed once and for all.

All past attempts to do this have been heartbreaking. The last failed attempt was so devastating that I had a small emotional breakdown. After the hospital team removed the trach and some time had passed with Lauren dozing quietly in her crib, her pulse oximeter readings started to decline, buzzers went off, and she began to gasp for air. It was horrifying to see her struggle for air—and to watch the team put the dreaded trach back in.

That damned tube has become a symbol of all the terror, exhaustion, and stress we have lived with. As long as Lauren has it, we are on edge, because its failure could kill her. As long as she has it, no one other than a trained medical professional can or will want to take care of her for fear of not handling the tube properly. The stakes are high, and every time the hospital team tries and fails to remove Lauren's trach, it's another reminder that we are not in control of our lives. The day that the staff had to reinsert it, I fled the hospital alone midprocedure, leaving Jim there with his mom. I just couldn't take it anymore. We had been so hopeful that this would be it, and when it wasn't, the letdown was crushing. I raced home, took a sleeping pill, and crawled into bed, too tired of being at the mercy of others and of living in fear to do anything but shut down.

I wasn't proud of my behavior that day, but I knew that I had reached a breaking point. I needed that one afternoon to reset. By the next day, I was off the canvas and ready to keep fighting.

Now we're about to try this delicate procedure again. This time, it will be with an ear/nose/throat (ENT) doctor at a much nicer hospital in Center City Philadelphia. Lauren's christening is scheduled for mid-October, ten days from now. We are tense and anxious as we pack our overnight bags (if the trach does come out and Lauren can breathe easily on her own for several hours, she will need to stay overnight in the ICU pediatric unit for observation). On our drive to the city, we pray that this time is the charm.

We walk into the hospital humming with nervous energy. We walk up to the front desk to check in. The receptionist looks up our names and frowns.

"There has been a last-minute change, and Lauren cannot have her procedure this morning," she says. "An emergency situation came up and the doctor and the staff are now unavailable. We'll have to reschedule."

"When?" I ask, my stomach churning.

"I can't say right now," she says. "We'll be in touch."

Done with us, she turns her attention back to the papers on her desk. Not even an apology for our wasted time. Jim and I just look at each other: *Not again.*

"It's Lauren's feeding time," Jim says as we walk out of the office.

I look around. The corridor we're in is bright and sunny and lined with window seats and plants. "Let's just do it here," I say.

We sit and pull out the supplies, and as we feed Lauren, we talk about how tired we are of the callous treatment we have received over these past six months.

"Things are hard enough as it is," I say. "And when they're thoughtless like this . . . it makes it so much worse."

Jim squeezes my hand. "I know."

A well-dressed woman who's walking by stops to admire Lauren.

"Hi," she says. "What a beautiful baby girl!"

Her attire and demeanor suggest that she is an important person at the hospital.

"I'm Grace Goodman, head of the volunteer board here," she says. She inspects us more closely. "Is everything okay?"

"Not exactly," I admit.

"Tell me about it," she encourages us, sitting down on the bench next to me.

After we share our story, she is concerned. "I'll speak with the ENT department on your behalf immediately," she says. "I'm appalled at the way you've been treated."

My goodness, where did this angel come from? She's definitely a hospital VIP, because she immediately obtains a new appointment for us and then gives me her personal commitment that she will be involved with its planning. She hands me her card and asks that I follow up with her next week, and also one day before the procedure date, to ensure that everything is set.

I am flabbergasted by this small miracle. There it is, another angel moment—just when we felt things couldn't be worse, Mrs. Goodman showed up and saved the day. It's a miracle that she appeared and advocated for us.

We are determined to not let the trach setback interfere with the joy of Lauren's christening. We will hide the damned trach under the dress collar, as we have been doing all along, when we take our christening photos. Still, we leave the hospital drained. The three of us take a long nap when we get home. Another day, shot. It's a struggle to remain optimistic about the future. I think about some of the new friends that we have met through the Arc. They have special needs toddlers, and their lives returned to "normal" once they stabilized the initial medical issues. I crave that kind of predictability the way a person lost in the desert craves water.

I make the mistake of returning to Dr. Fossett's office after he asks me to come back in to see him after my abrupt departure from our initial appointment. I think to myself, *I hope that he doesn't have the gall to ask me back to pay the co-pay that I walked out on from our first visit and to try to collect a second one for this visit, too.*

It seems that he and his staff were careful to schedule this appointment with me when no other patients were in sight. The parking lot and the office are empty. As we sit down in his office, Dr. Fossett complains that I have caused him trouble with the HMO and that he will reluctantly take Lauren as a patient. "Look, Mrs. Barker, I am sorry if we got off on the wrong foot here last time. But I wanted to be upfront with you about how your HMO coverage works. Harsh as it may seem, my practice is a business of care and for profit. I do need to keep an eye on my bottom line so that I am able to continue care for all of my patients. I don't appreciate your complaint about me to the HMO. But I understand that you have been through a lot these past few months and I am willing to take Lauren on as my patient."

I explode and give him a piece of my mind. "Dr. Fossett, I didn't come here today for your apology nor to ask for your forgiveness. It is obvious to me what your motives are, and I want no part of this game with you and the HMO. Not only will I never let you anywhere near my daughter, I am going to put together a comprehensive letter containing all that you've said to me and send it to the HMO. I'll also tell any parent that I meet about our encounter and your unprofessional behavior and lack of ethics. I will never forget this episode. And I want it to weigh on your conscience (if you have one) how harmful your behavior has been to me."

With that said, I leave his office in a huff, ignoring his receptionist on my way out. Once again, I drive down the road out of their sight, pull over, and have a huge cry over the terrible hurt that I feel. *Why, oh why, can't I find good, loving care for my precious baby girl who is so sweet and loving?* I cry for Lauren and not myself. I love her so much, and after all that she has suffered through, I want the best for her. I will press on and do whatever it takes to get her the proper care. *Please, God, help me to find someone good to take care of my special little girl.*

I must scramble fast to find a new pediatrician. With Lauren's precarious medical conditions, we need a primary physician as our point person and to authorize the ongoing specialist appointments. The next candidate is Dr. Sharkey, whom Roz, the Arc social worker has recommended. When I meet with him, I decide not to mention anything about my experience with Dr. Fossett and hope that they don't know each other. I simply state that, due to our recent move, we need a new local pediatrician.

I had given Dr. Sharkey some preliminary info about Lauren during our initial phone call, and I have asked that a copy of her records be sent to him from our original birth pediatrician and from the hospitals. I decide that it would be best to meet with him alone, without Lauren, so that I can focus solely on our conversation.

I want to be able to gauge his attitude and reactions to reading Lauren's thick medical file and to discuss his thoughts about her near-future care plan. From our meeting, I sense that he is a caring, competent doctor and appears to have no qualms about the high level of care that Lauren may need. Despite being an HMO practice, he doesn't seem fazed by the potential "liability" of Lauren's care, like Dr. Fossett was. He explains that he has a thriving practice with another doctor and a nurse practitioner on staff and that one patient with special needs will not be a problem for him. I still think that it is best to say nothing about my prior experience with Dr. Fossett. *Why upset the apple cart now, all seems good.*

"Dr. Sharkey, I've been told by other special needs parents that sometimes the HMO can discourage referrals to specialists or second opinions outside of the primary care doctor's office," I say. "So, with all of Lauren's needs for specialist visits, you are not concerned by this?"

"Mrs. Barker, that is not my worry. Lauren's intense needs are temporary. Hopefully soon she will be weaned from her trach, and then the G-tube feeding won't be necessary once the trach is gone. I feel confident, based on past patient histories, that this is a short-term need and that soon, other than her underlying heart condition, she will be fine."

I find his words comforting and caring. At the conclusion of this visit, I decide that he will be Lauren's new pediatrician

I tell him about the upcoming ENT appointment and how anxious we are to have the trach gone. He agrees that if the trach can be removed, Lauren will likely eat and drink more, and that will lead to the removal of her G-tube.

Dr. Sharkey seems to understand what our goals are. We set an appointment for him to meet and examine Lauren. I leave his office feeling reenergized. *Finally, a doctor I feel I can trust.*

Lauren's christening day was perfect—a lovely, sunny day—and we loved celebrating with our friends and family . . . but we weren't entirely present, because we were too busy looking forward to what was to come in two days later: the appointment where Lauren would finally (we hoped) have her trach tube removed once and for all. We've been able to think of little else for the past couple of weeks.

Mrs. Goodman has proven true to her word. I called her yesterday, and she assured me that we are all set. And this morning, when we arrive at the ENT suite, she is waiting for us. She greets us warmly and makes a big fuss over Lauren.

In the pediatric ICU, we undress Lauren and put her into one of the baby hospital gowns. Dr. Zwiller, the ENT specialist, apologizes about the emergency and confusion at our last visit. Lauren is sedated slightly, to keep her calm, and put on intravenous fluids, as she will not be able to drink for a while.

Taking the trach out is not a big procedure; it's just like changing it, except that it stays out. It's more about what happens after they take it out. The staff will need to keep a close eye on her breathing and her oxygen level. It's basically a waiting game to see if she can breathe on her own for a certain number of hours.

We try to keep Lauren calm by talking, singing, and reading picture books to her. The first hour passes: she is breathing fine. We are holding our breath, though.

"Why don't you have her sit up now," Dr. Zwiller suggests.

We carefully help her into a sitting position. She continues to breathe without difficulty.

"You can hold her now," Dr. Zwiller finally says.

I cradle her in my arms, and Lauren breathes fine. I feel like jumping for joy. *Good-bye, trach!*

After a few hours, Jim and I need to take a break. We head to the hospital cafeteria for a quick bite. When we come back, Lauren is sleeping peacefully. We sit by her crib so she'll see us as soon as she wakes up.

When she awakens, she wants to play. We gladly oblige and the afternoon passes quickly with our excitement. We sense that Lauren knows what is happening, too. The staff will likely want her to go to bed at her normal bedtime, about 8:30 p.m., so we get her into her pajamas and rock her to sleep with a story and a song. We leave the hospital tired but happy.

Being at the hospital is surprisingly exhausting. The atmosphere is tense, the air is stale, and the fluorescent lights strain the eyes. We hurry home to rest so we can be back bright and early tomorrow.

We sleep well. Our alarm awakens us; the night has passed without a phone call from the hospital, which is great news. Unless something crushing happens this morning, Lauren will be coming home by lunchtime.

We arrive at the hospital in time to give Lauren her breakfast via her G-tube. We are encouraged to have her drink by mouth, too. I have been working with Lauren for weeks, coaxing her to take food and drink by mouth despite the trach, as her therapists have recommended. Little by little, she has begun to ingest more by mouth, but not enough to sustain her. Baby steps.

Oddly, Dr. Zwiller does not stitch the trach hole closed.

"It will heal on its own," he says. "Just keep a Band-Aid over the area for the first week, and it should be fine."

I inspect the hole and see that it already looks smaller. Amazing.

"Further down the line, if you want to, you can have it cosmetically improved," Dr. Zwiller says. It's nice to know—but that's for later. We've had our fill of hospitals for now.

I've shipped Lauren's breathing apparatus back to the medical supply company—*good riddance!*—now that her trach is gone. This makes her therapy at the ARC easier. But all is not perfect. She still has the ugly, cumbersome G-tube, and because she is in diapers and does not walk or sit up well, there is always stress on her belly, whether she is lying on the floor or propped up in her little seat. The tube is stitched to the side of her stomach, and those stitches are breaking.

The tube also leaks what looks a lot like vomit out of the hole in Lauren's abdomen. This has been happening frequently after a feeding, and while it horrifies onlookers, it is even more traumatic for me and Lauren. I'm certain that the skin around the G-tube hole is irritated and painful. It makes me sick to think that my daughter could be in constant pain from it. I'm also worried that she is not getting enough nutrition.

On top of everything else, we have to be concerned about respiratory infections. Because she had a trach tube in it for six months, Lauren's airway is unusually sensitive. As cold and flu season has descended, Lauren has developed croup on a number of occasions. The first episode was frightening. She woke with a terrible, dry cough that sounded as if she were croaking.

We immediately gave her a breathing treatment with a drug that dilated her bronchial tubes, enabling her to breathe more easily. But we thought it would be wise to take her to see Dr. Sharkey to rule out any other problems—and that was when I discovered the downside of going to a pediatrician who has a "thriving" practice. Each time I've taken Lauren there, the waiting room has been full of coughing, sneezing, and feverish children. Even with an appointment, I sometimes sit in that germ-infested waiting room for over an hour.

Today, Lauren and I wait for two hours before getting in to see Dr. Sharkey, which is inexcusable. I'm beginning to think that we are being discriminated against because of Lauren's disability and her vulnerabilities, and also because of our miserly HMO insurance coverage. Regardless, it is depressing to feel so powerless and despised.

When we finally get into the exam room, I feel compelled to tell Dr. Sharkey how I'm feeling.

"We've been waiting to see you for two hours," I say. "I feel like we're not a priority. We were literally the last people to be seen this afternoon from your very full waiting room. I can't imagine that all of those people had an appointment scheduled prior to us. Why did this happen?"

He grew impatient. "Mrs. Barker, it is cold and flu season now, and this is traditionally our busiest time of year."

"Yes," I respond, "I can understand that, Doctor, but why were an entire roomful of patients seen before us? With Lauren's fragile health and her open trach, it isn't a wise idea for us to sit among so many coughing and sneezing children with germs literally flying in the air." I reminded him about our initial consultation, where I told him all about Lauren. I explained that I was a committed and devoted mother who wanted her daughter to be well as soon as possible and that I did not want to be here in his office any more than I had to be.

It's a standoff—another in a long list of wearying battles I've had to fight to ensure that my daughter gets the best possible care. After that visit, my gut was churning again. I silently prayed that this wasn't going to be the norm for our visits to his office. Ugh, I am beginning to feel that we are being spurned by these doctors.

I've gotten used to being exhausted, but one day a few weeks ago—about three weeks after "Trach Tube Liberation Day"—I found myself feeling even more run down than usual, and I realized that my last period had not entirely come to an end. It had slowed down, but I was still having some spotting—and some cramping, which I usually experience only at the onset of my cycle and never at the end. I had been so busy caring for Lauren and dealing with her needs that it had taken me a while to realize how long this has gone on.

No, it can't be. Not now.

Finally, after almost three weeks of this, I set an appointment to see my ob-gyn team in Phoenixville. I figure it's a good thing anyway, since I have not seen them for quite a while. They are the ones who signed off on my receiving disability leave, and it will soon be time for them to discuss if I am capable of returning to work. With the trach gone, Lauren's care is more manageable, but since the G-tube has become more problematic, I don't feel ready to send her to a day-care center. I don't think I'd be able to find one that would want to deal with the tube—and even if I could, I wouldn't trust them to care for it when it leaks.

When I get to the office, my gynecologist takes notes of my symptoms and draws blood and urine.

"Is there any chance that you're pregnant?" he asks.

"With all that has been going on in our lives, I'd say it's a slim chance, but I suppose it's a possibility," I reply. Because I am almost thirty and want to have more children, I did not go back on birth control pills after I became pregnant with Lauren. But Jim and I haven't been actively trying to get pregnant again; we've been too overwhelmed to think about having another child.

"Well, we won't know anything for sure until we get these test results back," he says. "We'll call you tomorrow and let you know what they say."

I am, indeed, pregnant. But my hormone levels seem odd, and it is not a good sign that I've been cramping and bleeding for weeks, so after the initial test results, my ob-gyn asked me to come back in for an exam and more blood tests.

My emotions have been a mess in the days since I found out I'm pregnant. On one hand, I am overjoyed about being pregnant again. I definitely want more children, regardless of all that we have gone through. I have always dreamed of having two or three children— and I think it will be good for us and for Lauren, too. As a child, she will have playmates; when she becomes an adult, she will have siblings to care for her once we are gone.

On the other hand, I worry about my ability to handle the demands of pregnancy with the daily stress of Lauren's care. *But nine months from now, Lauren will likely be rid of her G-tube and her intense medical issues,* I tell myself. *She might even be walking! Things will be easier then.*

But today, after my follow-up appointment and tests, my doctors advise me that this is not a normal pregnancy.

"It may be an ectopic pregnancy," my doctor tells me, a look of concern on his face.

"Ectopic?" I ask.

"It's when a fertilized egg gets stuck in a fallopian tube instead of traveling into the uterus. If the embryo starts to grow there, the result can be fatal to both the mother and the developing fetus," he explains. "And the tube can be damaged, which might make it harder for you to become pregnant in the future. If this is indeed an ectopic pregnancy, the embryo will have to be removed."

I sit, stunned, for just a moment. *Removed?*

But then there's no more time to be in shock. Because my ob-gyn's offices are located right next to the hospital in Phoenixville, they are able to squeeze me in to the ultrasound department right away, and there they confirm what they suspected: it's an ectopic pregnancy.

Sad as I am, these results are something of a relief. Another baby so close in age to Lauren just doesn't seem like a great idea. Her care still causes me a great deal of stress, and that is not conducive to a healthy pregnancy. Fate has brought me to where I am, and I need to accept it. There is no other option.

Because my ectopic pregnancy has been developing for more than a month already, my ob/gyn pressed for me to have my surgery immediately. I decided to have it done at the Philadelphia University hospital, and because my sisters have longstanding relationships with doctors there, I was able to get this coordinated right away.

We arranged for child care with family on the weekend days and with our nurses in the evenings, as usual. Because this was abdominal surgery and Lauren needs to be lifted, the HMO actually agreed to give me extra help during the day, when Jim is at work, for three weeks. They didn't even fight me on this round.

Thankfully, the surgery went as expected. But ever since I got home a couple of days ago, I've felt depressed. I am happy to be home, to see Lauren and my family, but the sadness and disappointment of these past months are coming to a head. I don't want to get out of bed. I cry at the slightest provocation. I know Jim and our family are beginning to worry about my mental health and the toll the relentless stress is taking on me.

This bed rest is the first time in nine months I've had the time to get off the merry-go-round and think about everything. It is a shock to stop and reflect on everything that has transpired. I'm worried about how low I'm feeling—I love Lauren, and I don't want to be deemed unfit to care for her—but I am just so darn tired after all that has gone wrong and the many, many hurts we have endured. Life still feels as if it is spinning out of control. No matter what careful plans I make, they get squashed. The sometimes callous, uncaring behavior from a handful of the professionals that we've depended on has left me wounded and betrayed. Even the strangers who stare at Lauren, not meaning to cause hurt, feel like enemies right now. I keep wondering when it will all end.

The thing that pains me the most is how my baby has suffered, and likely will suffer, in the near future because of the G-tube—and, worse yet, the prospect of more heart surgery. Once we build up Lauren's health and she grows to a certain height and weight, she will need to have heart surgery again. It is a dreary prospect.

Looking back at my misfortunes over the past year, it seems surreal. How could my life have become so distorted from just twelve months ago, when I was joyously healthy and pregnant? Things will get better soon . . . won't they?

The Next Bend in the Road

My visiting nurse comes to see me and we talk extensively. It becomes clear that it's the lack of control, more than anything else, that's got me feeling blue and helpless. Lauren needs me to be strong and to act as her buffer for what lies ahead in her life. Strength is the best gift I can give her. I stop taking my pain pills and substitute ibuprofen. My head gets clearer. I commit to nothing but positive energy going forward.

During my postsurgical confinement, Lauren has not had much outdoor activity other than her therapy at the Arc. Because of this, her G-tube has not been troublesome the way it was when she was moving around more. Nor has she had a croup attack. As Christmas approaches, things smooth out.

I love the Christmas season. I usually go all out with decorations, baking, and everything else. It is our tradition to host both of our families at our house on Christmas Eve. When I was pregnant, Christmas with a new baby was something I really looked forward to. So many of my old dreams have fallen by the wayside—but this dream, at least, is going to come true.

I buy Lauren a pretty Christmas dress. I shop for baby Christmas gifts for the first time. I schedule a sitting at the Sears portrait studio, and put her in her new dress and shoes for the occasion. I savor every bit of it. I am more fatigued than usual, but I write it off to my surgery, some sleepless nights, and the added stress of the holiday.

Lauren is eating and drinking more by mouth every day. Our

goal is to wean her off the G-tube in the New Year. It's been in her stomach since August—a long time for an active, growing baby.

We enjoy a wonderful Christmas Eve and Christmas Day. But a few days after Christmas, Lauren wakes up with a really bad case of croup. The nebulizer doesn't calm it, and I am afraid of her being unable to breathe. Reluctantly, we take her to the local hospital where Dr. Sharkey is on staff. He has become more unpleasant to deal with since Lauren began having issues with her leaky G-tube and since she started getting croup so frequently.

I am not happy that we are not at a children's specialty hospital, but we have no choice. Damned HMO rules! In just a few days, at the start of the New Year, I am free to switch health plans—and I am definitely changing! I don't care about the cost. My HMO is aging me prematurely. *I'll look for a new pediatrician, too,* I think as I brace myself for another exchange with Dr. Sharkey.

At this general hospital, Lauren is in a regular room, not an ICU. This seems very unwise for a baby with a breathing problem, but I defer to the doctors. Anyway, we will be here all day to monitor her, and she will be alone only if we go home to sleep. She is hooked up to an oxygen mist machine with some medicine that is supposed open her bronchial tubes. However, this medicine seems to agitate Lauren; she appears to be hyperventilating, and I can feel her heart racing as I pick her up and touch her little chest. She calls out constantly to me, "Ma, Ma, Ma," over and over again. It is heartbreaking.

"Is this normal?" I ask a kindly nurse named Kathy. "Her heart is beating so fast—it's like she's on speed or something."

"Actually, this medicine is a bit like speed," she says. "It's very effective, but it is important to be prudent with the dosage—especially in Lauren's case, given her heart condition. I'll ask Dr. Sharkey to reduce the dosage right away."

For two straight days, we stay all day with our girl. Jim tries to sleep at the hospital one night but can't. There are too many disruptions. Finally, we decide to stay each day until 10:00 p.m., go home to sleep, and come back early in the morning. We can't bear the thoughts of our little baby alone in a hospital room and in a hospital that has no pediatric specialists on staff, but we're no good to her if we're exhausted.

On the third morning, nurse Kathy comes into Lauren's room, closes the door, and nervously whispers that she needs to tell us something important.

"This is off the record, okay?" she says.

Jim and I exchange glances and nod.

"Lauren had a severe reaction to her medicine last night," she says, "to the point that she seemed about to go into cardiac arrest."

My stomach rises into my throat. *"What?"*

"I was so worried that I called for an emergency team," Kathy continues in a low voice.

This is horrifying! She is clearly implying that this hospital is *not* the place for our child. The tone of her voice and her expression tell us everything we need to know. If she were not on duty last night, Lauren might have died.

I'm almost unable to speak. I'm so grateful to Kathy for stepping in—I know this is another angel moment for us—but my gratitude is overshadowed by my outrage. Why would Dr. Sharkey insist on keeping the dosage of the medicine so high if Kathy told him Lauren was reacting badly to it? And why the hell, with her medical history, is Lauren in this second-rate local hospital instead of a specialized pediatric hospital to begin with? What do we have to do to get competent care with this HMO? I feel like screaming out loud in frustration. Why is my daughter receiving second-rate care? Are they prejudiced toward her because of her Down syndrome? Do they think that her life is not worth living?

This episode is another beating and another lesson learned. We can't trust anyone other than ourselves to care for and advocate for our child. Nurse Kathy's being on duty that night saved Lauren's life. This was indeed another angel moment.

❇ ❇

When Lauren awakes, her croup is better, and we request her discharge as soon as possible. It's almost the New Year. Only two more days until we can say good-bye to this rubbish HMO.

Prior to discharge, I ask about the possibility of removing the G-tube once and for all, since Lauren is capable of eating by mouth now. The worst-case scenario is that we would have to go back to the NG tube, and I would prefer that—it is less invasive and far less traumatic. I regret that I ever allowed this G-tube to be inserted into Lauren's stomach in the first place. The accompanying complications were not adequately explained to us prior to its placement. When they proposed this surgery as a better solution for Lauren's feeding, my gut told me no, but I ignored it. Now I know I should have followed my instincts about my baby's needs. This G-tube has turned out to be a setback, not a help. It's another harsh life lesson learned. I need to trust my instincts more. I am waking up to the reality that modern medicine and doctors are not always right. It is important to know your body, to feel its instincts, and to pay just as much attention to them as you're paying to the facts when you make your decisions.

We have found out from other parents of Down syndrome children that we've met at the Arc that they managed fine with the simple nasal tube feeding until their baby ate better orally, and the babies progressed to eating orally faster than Lauren has. I've never met another parent of a Down syndrome baby whose child has had a G-tube put in, in fact. It seems that once again, we got terrible advice. When the G-tube leaks, Lauren actually loses weight!

Dr. Sharkey agrees to our request, and he removes the tube before we depart. Like the trach tube removal, it is a minor procedure.

"The holes in Lauren's stomach will heal on their own," Dr. Sharkey says. "We don't need to sew them closed."

"Really?" I ask, a bit skeptical. I know her trach hole closed on its own, but the G-tube doesn't seem like something we can just cover with a Band-Aid and be done with.

"Really," he says firmly. "It will heal just fine on its own."

Because we don't know any better, we trust his word on this. But in the days that follow, we discover that he is wrong. Lauren's stomach holes are not just closing up and healing like her trach hole did, and we have to go back to the hospital to learn how to bind her stomach with bandages and some temporary adhesives to fix it.

The trach hole didn't seem to be painful at all to Lauren, but this stomach wound that won't heal leaks acidic fluids out onto Lauren's tender abdominal skin. This G-tube has proved to be just as troublesome and scary, perhaps worse, than Lauren's trach was for care. I panic every time it begins to leak stomach fluids, and I feel heartbroken when I see her cringe from it. She is losing valuable nutrition with this awful stomach leaking. She looks thinner. And although her tolerance for discomfort is high after all that she has endured, I can tell that this leaking hurts her.

"When will this pain and misery end for my poor baby?" I ask out loud. "Please, God, give her a break."

There is something positive that accompanies all this pain, however: with my three weeks of surgical recovery time done and with Lauren's G-tube out, we need no more nighttime nursing care. No more strangers in our home each evening—hooray!

I put in a call to Oak Grove Pediatric group to set an appointment with Dr. Linda Barnett, my sister Rose's pediatrician. We'll see her in two weeks. In the meantime, we settle in to rest up from the holidays.

"Lauren will need surgery to properly close her stomach hole," Dr. Barnett says at our first visit with her.

She doesn't say anything to directly contradict our former pediatrician, but I sense that she is wondering why the heck Dr. Sharkey let this wound fester and leak for weeks when a simple procedure would close it safely.

"She will need to be intubated during surgery, but it's a minor procedure that should involve only one overnight stay," she says. "Nothing to worry about."

While this news is something of a relief, I am ready to curse the entire medical profession, starting with Dr. Sharkey. Clearly, he should have ordered this surgery weeks earlier to save Lauren the pain and suffering of her festering wound. He also skimped by choosing to admit her into the local hospital, which was ill equipped to deal with her croup. He has proved to be a huge disappointment, and we're glad to bid him good riddance. Hindsight is always twenty-twenty; a lesson we seem to be learning over and over these past nine months.

It is difficult to fight with your caregivers if you are stuck with them because of an HMO. It disgusts me that our precious daughter's life has been put at risk for the sake of cost savings. Never again!

The surgery goes well and Lauren comes home—no trach, no G-tube. It's a joyous event. But our work isn't done; now we need to teach her to eat and drink.

Because Lauren missed the ability to suck a bottle, we are advised to have her drink from a sippy cup. This takes persistence. Sipping and swallowing are not instinctive for Lauren because of the months with her trach and G-tube. But we keep at it. We have help with this important task from the speech therapist from the Arc program. She give us instruction as to what we need to do at mealtime. Simple, but important steps. So at each mealtime, Lauren sits in her high chair with us at the table. We take a sippy cup ourselves and in slow motion and with great enthusiasm, we exaggerate ourselves drinking from this cup. Lauren does indeed watch us carefully doing this. Simultaneously, we also hold her little hand to our throat so that she can feel us gulping and swallowing as we drink. We then offer her her own sippy cup and encourage her to drink and also lightly touch her throat as she does to imitate what we were doing previously. It's time consuming, but it works. Lauren learns to drink from the cup. I am sure that some of this is natural survival instinct kicking in. Whatever the reason, we are happy that it is working.

But while Lauren is improving, I am becoming concerned about my health. My fatigue, which has been present since my surgery, is worsening. My appetite is poor. My eyes seem constantly bloodshot, and my bowel movements aren't normal. I make an appointment with my ob-gyn's office, where I describe my symptoms and they take blood and urine. They tell me that they will send the report to my primary care doctor, Dr. Simpson, in Phoenixville.

When I arrive at Dr. Simpson's office, I am immediately put in an exam room by his nurse. I am so tired that I lie back on the exam table and am half asleep when Dr. Simpson comes in.

I sit up when I hear the door open. I can tell by his face that something is amiss. *Now what?*

"How are you, Liz?" he asks.

"Tired," I say. "I'm tired all the time lately."

He examines me, particularly my skin and my eyes, and asks about my bowel movements and eating habits. He then sits and drops the bomb.

"I'm sorry to tell you this, but you have hepatitis B," he says.

I blanch. "Hepatitis?"

He explains that there are three types of hepatitis—A, B and C. "C is the worst," he says, "so it's good you don't have that. But hepatitis B is not so easily contracted; you can only get it as you would get HIV: via intimate contact with an affected person, blood transfusion, drug needles, or surgery mishaps."

I am shocked and a bit embarrassed. But Dr. Simpson knows that I am not a drug user, and we share a laugh at the idea that I would have time to fool around sexually with my insane home life demands, which makes me feel a bit better.

"Given when these symptoms began to manifest," he finally says, "I'm almost certain that you contracted the hepatitis during your ectopic pregnancy surgery."

"How in the world could this have happened?" I ask.

"It doesn't happen often," he replies, "but no one is infallible, and mistakes can happen in hospitals."

Don't I know it.

"Where do we go from here?" I ask.

Dr. Simpson tells me that the first thing to do is to test Jim to see if he has hepatitis B. If he doesn't, that strengthens the hypothesis that I contracted it from the hospital during my surgery. He also advises that we test Lauren as well. It is a simple blood draw. It would also be a good idea, he suggests, to talk to the surgeon to inquire if there were other surgical patients from that day who have come down with these symptoms.

I recall my surgeon saying that he had several surgeries that morning and that I was the last one, an emergency "add-on." Perhaps with all of the activity that morning in that OR, something was not sterilized carefully, or something was contaminated. It's right in line with the way my luck has been running these past eleven months. I should move to Las Vegas and make a living as a cooler, one of those people with bad luck who the casinos call to put the whammy on a gambler's hot streak. What are the odds of me catching someone else's disease in a reputable hospital with a reputable doctor?

As I'm thinking about this, Dr. Simpson catches my attention with another piece of news: "I should tell you that there is no cure for hepatitis B," he says.

"No cure?" I repeat. "What does that mean?"

"Well, it doesn't mean that you'll always feel this way," he rushes to assure me. "But it does mean that there is no medicine to treat it. The only treatment is to allow the body to rest and heal itself over time. The hepatitis B antigen never leaves the body; it simply becomes dormant."

Dr. Simpson goes on to explain the other consequences of having this disease: I will forever be prohibited from donating blood. I should be cautious about alcohol or other substances in the future that may affect my liver. For the rest of my life, I will now have to disclose the fact that I have hepatitis B to any physician who treats me.

I feel like I'm branded with a scarlet letter. I worry that this diagnosis may raise eyebrows for those who don't know me. For now, though, it is the least of my items on my long "worry list."

Dr. Simpson concludes by saying that I should not return to work at this time. "It would be too taxing on your already weakened immune system," he states. "It's evident that you are fatigued from caring for Lauren's special needs, and that fatigue is being compounded by your hepatitis. I strongly suggest that you take more time to build your strength, and minimize undue stress whenever possible." His face grows serious. "If you do not give yourself time to rest and recuperate, there is a danger that the disease could worsen. If that were to happen, your liver could be permanently damaged, which could be life threatening."

Rest and no stress? Sure, that's my life, doc! I can barely believe what I'm hearing. It's not Dr. Simpson's doing, but once again I feel betrayed by the health-care system. I have spent the past year going through a series of hospitals and doctors who sometimes seem to care nothing for my baby, and now I have become permanently ill with a disease that I strongly suspect was transmitted to me while I was under a hospital's care. I am spiraling down into a vortex of self-pity—but then I stop myself. *Remember Lauren,* I remind myself. *Remember your vow to focus only on the positive from now on.*

I decide that I will look at this glass as half full. Because of my hepatitis B, I will have more time at home with Lauren, and that is a positive thing. This compulsory respite from returning to work will give us both a chance to heal and to bond more deeply.

I leave Dr. Simpson's office surprisingly relieved. I know my diagnosis; I'm very glad my problems are not psychological. I have been given official permission to take the time to take care of myself and rest, as best as I can, while caring for Lauren. I intend to investigate how I contracted this disease, of course—if it did happen during my surgery, I want to hold the hospital responsible for it—but I'm looking forward to spending quality time with my daughter for the next two months. These negatives I've experienced in the past couple of months—my ectopic pregnancy and now my hepatitis— are actually positive in a strange, twisted way. They have bought us more time for the nursing care for Lauren and for me to stay home. Our extended time together now might make up for those long five months in the cold hospital setting where we were apart. It's like taking a bullet for my child—twice. And out of love, I'd do it all over again for her if I had to.

New Normal

As I drive the forty-five minutes back to the Arc Alliance to pick up Lauren after my appointment with Dr. Simpson, I am more relaxed than I have been in months. Lauren's health is stable, for now, and I have essentially been given a pass to take some time for myself to heal. I deflect my thoughts from my diagnosis to make a mental list of all of the things I need to accomplish in the coming weeks.

Top priority: make an appointment to see the surgeon at Philadelphia University hospital about my hepatitis. Then establish a relationship with a new physician in our area for Jim and me. Though I like Dr. Simpson, the drive is too far for routine care. Also, find a new ob-gyn; I won't go back to the Philadelphia University docs after this hepatitis disaster.

Next, I must update my disability status with my ever-understanding employer. I am confident that they will agree to extend my disability benefit given my recent diagnosis. I am grateful to work with such amazing people. They have been so helpful and supportive.

I also need to inquire about day care for Lauren for when I do return to work. She will be one year old by then. Previously, Lauren wasn't eligible even for special needs–friendly day care because of her trach and G-tube. The Arc Alliance is merely for therapies and is not a day care or preschool per se.

With all of these thoughts running through my head, the forty-five-minute drive back to the Arc flies by. I see Roz, the social worker, on my way in, and I figure I might as well knock one thing off my list.

"I'll be going back to work in a few months," I say. "Do you know if there are any good day cares in the area equipped to take care of a child with Lauren's needs?"

"The KenCrest organization has a preschool program for special needs children that's not too far away," she says. "We can call right now, if you'd like, to see if they have any spots open!"

I breathe out a sigh of relief. "Yes, that would be great!"

We call, and the program director, Kate, says there is an open spot and room for Lauren! I can only hope that the KenCrest facility and staff are as wonderful as the Arc.

Lauren is eating and drinking well now thanks to my work and lessons from her delightful speech therapist, Sheila, who comes to our home so that Lauren can work on her skills in her own kitchen, in her own high chair, and using her own sippy cup. Sheila has many useful tricks for encouraging Lauren to eat and drink that she is teaching me. She has even coaxed Lauren to speak more, too.

Babies with mild Down syndrome will do most of the things that "normal" babies do; it just takes them longer to do so. For example, Lauren is almost a year old, yet she is nowhere near walking because her muscles are not strong enough. She will likely walk at closer to eighteen months. She is crawling and pulling up as she should, however. I exercise her every day at home, as instructed by her therapists at the Arc. I also talk and sing to her, which isn't hard for a chatterbox like me. The next few months or so will be a great time to strengthen her body and her mind . . . and have some fun.

On to my priority list.

I join the pediatric and ob-gyn practices that my sister Rose goes to. I also decide to join a new family practice—the doctor, Tim Robinson, is young, but he came recommended by someone at the Arc, who told me what a warm and caring person he is. I want someone who will put my family's health before any other considerations. I know it's wishful thinking. *We'll see*, I think. Jim's blood test is negative, thankfully. He doesn't have hepatitis.

After just a few days of no strangers in my home, no medical episodes, and no worries about my job and disability and health insurance, I am feeling stronger and so much better. I am ready to face off with the Philadelphia University doctors about what happened on the morning of my surgery.

I get right to the point with Dr. Johannon.

"I have hepatitis B," I tell him, "and my husband and my child do not. Do you have any idea how I might have contracted it?"

"I have no idea," Dr. Johannon says, admitting nothing.

"My doctor thinks it probably happened during my surgery," I say. "The timing lines up with when I started experiencing the symptoms."

He admits nothing. He says that I have no proof that infection occurred during surgery, and that it will be impossible to obtain any. He tells me that privacy laws prohibit him from discussing if other patients of his from that day are exhibiting signs of the disease.

I don't know why I expected anything else. Hospitals have policies in place to protect them from liability, even if disclosure is in the patient's best interest. HIPAA, the Health Insurance Portability and Accountability Act, prohibits them from revealing any information about other patients. It's a convenient excuse. Why is it okay to flag a restaurant that served tainted food to patrons but not okay to point the finger at a hospital that may have transmitted a dangerous disease to its patients? I thank God that I contracted hepatitis and not HIV, but who knows what else might show up in the future from this medical blunder. I don't want to dwell on that thought.

I leave the hospital angry and no closer to the answers I'm looking for. I decide to contact an attorney to investigate on my behalf; I do not want to tax my health over this situation, but I don't want to drop the issue until I find out how I contracted this disease. Beyond that, I will move forward, as I must.

Over the following months, life begins to assume a rhythm that I can only describe as "normal." There's a notable lack of drama and crisis. Jim, Lauren, and I settle into a peaceful routine, something we've been missing for a long, long time. We become acquainted with our new physicians: Dr. Katz (ob-gyn), Dr. Barnett (pediatrics), and Dr. Robinson (general practice). I get good vibes from all of them and have my fingers crossed that they will live up to my expectations.

We visit KenCrest, where Lauren will go for day care when I return to work. Its day-care and learning centers are located in the downstairs part of a huge Lutheran church that has lovely windows that let in the sunlight. The rooms are bright and cheerful and filled with toys, books, scooters, and ride-ons. Kate, who runs KenCrest, is a pleasure, as is her staff of teachers and aides. They greet Lauren warmly and invite her to sit in a song circle during our visit. She loves it and claps her hands with joy. The vibe here could not be more positive and energetic. *This is perfect,* I think.

We complete enrollment paperwork. Since I don't yet have to return to work, Lauren will attend only part-time for now. This will allow her to integrate this new change into her life gradually. I'll also be able to go back to work for about thirty hours per week—a compromise that will allow me to retain my benefits without resuming my job full-time.

After almost one year of hell, normal life seems to be resuming. Feeling reinvigorated and with my hepatitis symptoms abating as I relax, I decide we should take a trip to Florida—an early Mother's Day present to myself, since last year's Mother's Day was so miserable. Jim and I are both excited for this wonderful opportunity to experience what we initially missed as a young family: quality family time, just the three of us together enjoying one another.

The trip is bliss. There are no travel mishaps, medical incidents, or stress. The people at the hotel thoughtfully give us a ground-level, beachfront room. This allows Jim and me to relax on our room's little patio, or sit on the beach in front of our room, with the patio door open while Lauren naps so that we can hear her. This past year had been so stressful. The spring and summer were consumed with

Lauren's hospitalization, and the winter season was anxiety ridden with trach, G-tube, croup, and pediatrician challenges. After these long, hard months, it is exhilarating to feel relaxed and free of worry about medical issues. *Free to be, you and me* pops into my head. When we first fling open our room's patio door, I step out onto the beach holding Lauren. I twirl and dance with her in my arms and sing, "Free to be us, Lauren, you and me." Lauren loves it when I sing to her. "It's our time to have fun, baby girl." Yes, we can now be the little family I had envisioned while I was pregnant.

We return home refreshed. I am finally going back to work. We have daytime child care set. We can even take advantage of "respite time" to go out in the evening, knowing that we'll have access to trained babysitters for eight hours per month. One in particular, Jinny Leith, is a gem. She lives five minutes from us and is an assistant director for Easter Seals. Because she is single and has no children, she enjoys spending time with other families, especially those with special needs children. What a godsend she is. We develop a close friendship with not only Jinny but also her family. In particular, her niece Chris, who is a nurse at our local hospital.

In our new neighborhood, we meet Sal and Mary Ricco (our next-door neighbors on one side) and Barbara and Buzz Brown (our next-door neighbors on the other side); across the street are Mary and Ed Cramer. On walks with Lauren in her stroller, I meet several women with young children about Lauren's age. At long last, we are settling into our life—the life we've dreamed of. We are new parents doing fun things with our child, without pesky things like hospitals and health concerns getting in the way.

The life we've had the past year feels like something out of a bad reality show—something lived by actors—but Lauren and I have emerged both changed and stronger. My disease is dormant. Lauren is healing and progressing, albeit at a slower pace than other babies her age might. And we've finally escaped from the insurance and medical maze that has trapped and confused us for the past year.

We attend monthly support group meetings for the Arc Alliance and the Down Syndrome Interest Group. At the Down syndrome group, many of the discussions revolve around what life may be like for our children as they grow and mature to adults. How can we gauge our children's intelligence level, emotional maturity, and overall capabilities compared to norms? How do we keep their minds and bodies active and healthy with sports, exercise, and extracurricular activities? They are cute and adorable now, but what happens when they grow into adolescents and adults but still have the minds of children? How difficult will it be to teach them social skills and eating and dressing habits? Will they be able to have jobs and live independently?

The long-term issues are weighty and important, but I am thinking more near term. Specifically, the second heart surgery Lauren will need when she is three or four years old. This line of thought sparks a discussion between Jim and me about having more children. It would be very good for Lauren to have brothers and sisters. It feels like we're getting to a place where that might be a possibility.

We spend the summer swimming in our backyard pool, taking day trips to parks, and going to Uncle Jeff's lake house on weekends. Fall brings school trips to a pumpkin patch and Halloween costume parties. Thanksgiving and Christmas are the highlights of the year. Life is good again. We are in high spirits. And Lauren is thriving. Her nickname is "the Little Imp" because she has an impish smile and is so friendly. As people pass us in store aisles, she always says, "Hi!" If they don't initially respond, she keeps saying it until they do. I find this amazing. Despite all of the awful and painful things she's had to endure, she retains her cheerful personality. She is such a happy and content child. Her sweetness endears her to everyone who knows her. At school, she is a favorite of her teachers and therapists because of her sunny personality.

Buoyed by the peace and harmony that have reentered our lives, Jim and I book another trip to Florida and begin trying to get pregnant again.

Well, fertility isn't a problem. A few weeks after we return home from Florida, I realize that I am pregnant. This time, there are no unusual symptoms. But after all that we have gone through, we decide that we will take advantage of a new in utero fetal genetic test called chorionic villus sampling, or CVS, which is newer and less invasive than amniocentesis testing. Amniocentesis testing requires a doctor to carefully stick a needle through your abdomen and into the fetal sac to draw some amniotic fluid, all without sticking or harming the developing fetus. There is a risk of accidentally aborting the pregnancy. CVS, on the other hand, is a deep vaginal exam where the doctor scrapes a sample of cells from the fetal sac without actually penetrating it. It can be done a few weeks later than amniocentesis, which allows the pregnancy to stabilize first.

We decide to keep our new bundle of joy a secret until we can have the CVS test and get the results—around the fourteen-week point of my pregnancy. We also decide that we want to know the sex of the new baby, although we won't share that with anyone. We just want to be able to do some behind-the-scenes planning in case something develops with Lauren's health that requires our attention later in the pregnancy.

When we receive the CVS results, we get happy news: our new baby is healthy. And we are expecting a boy! My due date is pegged for December 17—not a great time to be giving birth, what with the inevitably busy holiday schedule, but no matter. Everybody is healthy! We decide to name our son James Joseph Barker IV in honor of Jim's dad and grandfather.

Over the coming months, Lauren grows physically and develops mentally to the point that I suspect she is high functioning. But while she is the appropriate height and weight for her age, two and a half, it is becoming apparent that she needs the heart surgery. Although she can walk, she can't run far. This is partially due to impaired coordination, but it's largely because her heart can't keep up with her bigger body. She is also extremely sensitive to heat and cold. We were told from the outset that Lauren would likely need another heart surgery as she grew. Now it looks like this dreaded time has come.

Welcome to Holland

Lauren is scheduled for a catheterization in mid-September to check the condition of her heart. She will have to stay overnight afterward as a precaution. We dread going back to the dreary William Penn Hospital and to the inner city Badlands. Although our health insurance coverage was switched away from the stingy HMO plan and we are no longer bound to William Penn, we are confident with Lauren's cardiologist there. Dr. Ronald Dawson sees Lauren every 4 months and he is a good doctor. He is one of the doctors that I get good vibes from. I sense his genuine care for Lauren. In fact, Dr. Dawson encourages us to have Lauren's surgery there because the hospital recently recruited a well know pediatric heart surgeon from the mid-west to its staff. And so, although we dislike the hospital's location, we are reluctant to make a change and to explore the option of CHOP. We feel that this hospital's staff knows Lauren's history and despite its shabbiness, it pulled Lauren through after her dramatic newborn surgery.

In retrospect, we will understand that we were offered an angel moment here at this critical juncture, that we unfortunately did not heed. As we debated about getting a second opinion at CHOP, Jim's mother came forth to tell us about a chance encounter and conversation that she had with a woman whose child had heart surgery there. The woman said that the doctor's last name was the same as the private grade school that Jim attended, a school that she felt was especially good for Jim growing up. We blew off this tip in favor of our comfort factor.

In short order, we'd realize the mistake that we made and the jeopardy that would ensue.

The procedure goes well but confirms what we fear: Lauren will need more heart surgery, soon. If we delay too long, it could compromise her health.

"It's fine to wait until the New Year, after you have delivered," says Lauren's cardiologist, Dr. Dawson. "And you're in luck—we have a new, top-notch pediatric heart surgeon who recently joined us from the Mayo Clinic, Dr. Rollins. Lauren will be in good hands."

This will be a long and invasive surgery; Lauren will need an astounding sixteen units of blood in order to get through the procedure. "The HIV virus has been appearing in donated blood," he says, "so I suggest that you work with the Red Cross to mobilize your own blood donors, just to be safe."

Because of my hepatitis, I won't be able to donate blood for my own daughter, even though I share her A negative blood type. *If I can't do it, I'll find people who can,* I resolve.

Lauren's upcoming surgery puts a damper on our joy about our son's upcoming birth. Besides the fact that surgery is always scary, it's a reminder to us of the bad times that we wish could be behind us forever. But we try to block negative thoughts as we busily prepare for the holidays and the birth of our son.

After Thanksgiving, I stop working. I send about seventy-five letters to friends, family, coworkers, and staff at Lauren's programs about our "blood drive," trying to find out who might have type A negative blood and be able to donate. The response is extraordinary. People are eager to help, to literally give of themselves to help our precious daughter. The love that comes back to us is overwhelming. It soothes my nerves and lifts my spirits.

By December 10, I have all of my Christmas chores done: shopping, wrapping, decorating, and cards written. As my due date approaches, my weight gain makes me irritable; picking up and carrying Lauren becomes uncomfortable. On Friday, December 16, the

Arc Alliance has its Christmas party for the kids and their families, with Santa, lunch, presents, and some songs and games. While at the party, I start to feel crampy. After going to bed that evening, I wake up with sharp pains at about 5:00 a.m.

We don't call my parents immediately. As with my labor with Lauren, I don't expect to need to go to the hospital for a few hours. But labor progresses rapidly, and at 7:00 we call them to come over. My water has broken, and the pains are now very close together. We drive to the Oak Grove Hospital ER, only five minutes away, and within two hours, James is born.

The moment James enters the world, he is whisked to a nearby examining table to be cleaned up, tested, and have his lungs suctioned out, just to ensure that he did not swallow any fecal matter on his way out. Then the nurse hands him to his father.

Jim brings James close to me so that I may see him and kiss his forehead.

It is a huge relief that my labor and delivery has all gone so smoothly. To say that we are relieved, happy, and grateful is a gross understatement.

It is an indescribable thrill for me to hold newborn baby James. In some respects, I feel like a first-time mother. I missed all of these tender moments that I should have had with Lauren just after her birth because of her condition and medical "accessories."

Just to be sure, I focus my groggy eyes and scrutinize my new baby. I ask Jim, "Is he perfectly fine and okay?" Jim assures me that he is. I know that he is just as relieved as I am at this moment. For weeks, neither of us could say what we were secretly afraid of. We were both worried about a birthing mishap or any unexpected medical complications for our baby. Thankfully, there are none. Like Lauren, James was born with a full head of dark hair, and he is large and long as she was, too. He is almost ten pounds at birth and more than twenty-one inches long. He resembles Jim. As I hold him in my arms, I say over and over again, "Baby James, we love you so!"

My maternity leave will extend to just about the time when Lauren will enter the hospital for her surgery. I wonder how women who work full-time manage this: pulling themselves together for work while getting their children up, dressed, fed, in the car, and off to day care.

We have already moved Lauren into a new bedroom of her own. We call it her "big girl room," and she was intimately involved in the process of setting it up. She understands about the new baby coming into her "old baby crib." Because she loves *Sesame Street,* she and I buy bedding with these characters on it for her room. Watching the show with her, I learn that one of the show's writers, Emily Perl Kingsley, has a son, Jason, with Down syndrome, and that she has written extensively about their lives. One of my favorite writings of Emily's describes the experience of discovering that your baby has been born with special needs. It is called "Welcome to Holland."

"Welcome to Holland," by Emily Perl Kingsley

I am often asked to describe the experience of raising a child with a disability—to try to help people who have not shared that unique experience to understand it, to imagine how it would feel. It's like this . . .

When you're going to have a baby, it's like planning a fabulous vacation trip—to Italy. You buy a bunch of guidebooks and make your wonderful plans. The Coliseum. The Michelangelo. David. The gondolas in Venice. You may learn some handy phrases in Italian. It's all very exciting.

After months of eager anticipation, the day finally arrives. You pack your bags and off you go. Several hours later, the plane lands. The stewardess comes in and says, "Welcome to Holland."

"Holland?!?" you say. "What do you mean Holland? I signed up for Italy! I'm supposed to be in Italy. All my life I've dreamed of going to Italy."

But there's been a change in the flight plan. They've landed in Holland and there you must stay.

The important thing is that they haven't taken you to a horrible, disgusting, filthy place, full of pestilence, famine and disease. It's just a different place.

So you must go out and buy new guidebooks. And you must learn a whole new language. And you will meet a whole new group of people you would never have met.

It's just a different place. It's slower-paced than Italy, less flashy than Italy. But after you've been there for a while and you catch your breath, you look around . . . and you begin to notice that Holland has windmills . . . and Holland has tulips. Holland even has Rembrandts.

But everyone you know is busy coming and going from Italy . . . and they're all bragging about what a wonderful time they had there. And for the rest of your life, you will say, "Yes, that's where I was supposed to go. That's what I had planned."

And the pain of that will never, ever, ever, ever go away . . . because the loss of that dream is a very, very significant loss. But . . . if you spend your life mourning the fact that you didn't get to Italy, you may never be free to enjoy the very special, the very lovely things . . . about Holland.

This poem beautifully captures the emotions of parents confronted with the news of a special needs child—initially confusion and anger, and later, the unexpected beauty. At first, you're shocked by the injustice of the universe. You want to shake your fists at God and scream, "But it wasn't supposed to be this way!" Then you come to realize that this experience will be what you choose to make it— and if you choose to embrace it, it can transform you in ways that having a "normal" child never could.

But let's be frank, it's never easy. There are numerous extra considerations that grow weightier as the years pass and your sweet child grows and journeys into adulthood. Lauren is only two, and I feel that I have already experienced some of the prejudices aimed at her regarding her medical care. I pray that these are not just the tips of a huge iceberg that looms ahead in our future. I also pray that I will always be strong and well enough to advocate for my daughter.

I have to set up home child care for infant James while Lauren is in the hospital. Lauren's heart surgery will be serious and complex, and we are determined to be at the hospital with her every step of the way. In the past year, Jim has become self-employed, teaming up with two other partners to open a deli restaurant in Center City Philadelphia, so he does not have the option of disability leave or much vacation time. His day begins and ends early, though, so he will come over to William Penn Memorial each day immediately after work.

Roz at the Arc helps me find an agency whose specialty is home and overnight care for young children. Our caregiver will sleep in Lauren's room so she can care for James in case we have to go to the hospital at a moment's notice. For the critical first two weeks, we will have someone with us daily. If all goes well, Lauren will be stable after that and we can cut back and have more time with James.

As February 20, the day of Lauren's surgery, approaches, I try to think ahead to spring and her birthday in April. I think about planning a party to celebrate her health. Because I am anxious about Lauren's surgery, I am not lactating well and I all but abandon trying to breast-feed James, who is a very hungry baby. I nurse him only at the end of the day, as a comfort. I could use some comfort myself. When Lauren was born, I felt a bit cheated by not having the textbook new-mother experience. I missed so much in those first five months. And once again with baby James, it is a less than idyllic experience for both of us. During my last trimester with him, we were undergoing Lauren's heart catheterization and setting the plans for her major surgery. Now, in the New Year, I am a nervous wreck—scrambling for her blood drive, being cautious that she stays healthy pre-op, and working out elaborate planning for child and household care for the days Jim and I will be spending at the hospital with Lauren. It's no wonder I can't relax and allow my milk to flow as it should. I rationalize to myself that with James's birth weight, I'd likely need to supplement with a bottle anyway to keep him full.

The night before Lauren's surgery, we spend extra time with her.

"Tomorrow," I tell her, "we have to go to the hospital. They're going to fix your heart so that you can run better and faster."

She smiles. I am not sure if she understands, but I feel better having explained it. I stay an extra-long time in her room with her, read her several stories, and rock her to sleep in my arms. As I lay her down in her bed, I cry, knowing that she won't be in that bed again for at least two weeks. After tucking the blankets around her tiny body, I put both of my hands on her chest and pray that she will be fine and that the surgery will go well.

God, let my healthy energy transfer to her body, I pray. *Take what you need from me to make her stronger.* After ten minutes of this, I literally feel drained, as if my energy has been sucked right out of my body. I don't mind, though—not if it will help my precious Lauren survive and thrive. I go to bed exhausted, dreading tomorrow.

We leave the house at 9:00 a.m. and drive through the Badlands to William Penn Memorial, where Lauren is admitted to the cardiac care unit and put in her toddler hospital gown. We walk next to her gurney all the way down to the operating room door. We put on happy faces and hug her tightly. Then we settle into the CCU waiting room nearby. Once there, I burst into sobs. After the peace and the wonderful, happy times we've had with Lauren over the past eighteen months, this is the last place I want to be. So much can go wrong with this surgery and the recovery. I am so frightened that I am shaking inside. I force myself to think positively.

I have brought a project to keep me occupied: James's baby book. Once we christen him, I will have more to add, but we have deferred his christening until Lauren is well and strong. Working on this baby book is meant to be a simple and pleasurable diversion for me. It will allow me to reminisce about the many joys of James's birth—the baby shower, homecoming, photos, growth updates—and to dream about our future together. I anticipate that I'll work on this when we have downtime while Lauren is napping.

Two hours pass. A cardiac intern updates us: the surgery is proceeding pretty much as planned. Buoyed by that news, we run down to the cafeteria and grab lunch. When we return, however, it seems that the surgery is taking longer than expected, and no one offers us another update.

"Why aren't they telling us what's happening?" I ask Jim, getting worried.

He shakes his head. "I don't know."

"Should we go wait by the post-op room?" I say. I can't sit in this waiting room any longer.

Jim stands right away. "Yeah, let's go."

We walk down to the post-op room, and after hovering there for a couple of minutes, we catch a surgical staff member going out.

"We're Lauren's parents," I say, trying not sound too panicky. "We haven't gotten an update in a while . . . can you tell us what's happening?"

"She's in post-op," she says. "She's not fully awake yet, but she should be soon, and we'll bring her out."

Jim and I hug, relieved. "Thank you!" I say.

Ten minutes later, the doors open and Lauren is wheeled out.

"We're sorry about the delay," a young doctor says. "After Lauren's chest wound was stitched closed, a heart valve leak unexpectedly occurred. We had to open her up again to fix it."

Dr. Rollins shoots the young physician a stern look for sharing this information, and my radar is immediately on full alert.

"What happened, exactly?" I ask.

Dr. Rollins steps in. "It's not as bad as it sounds," he says abruptly. "These things happen sometimes."

We press for more information and receive only curt answers. But then our focus is on Lauren, who is trying to sit up. With her deep chest wound, she needs to be still.

"Shh, sweetie, it's okay," I soothe her, and she relaxes back in her bed. It is painful to see her drugged and bandaged, but at least she's not on a respirator—she's breathing on her own, albeit with an oxygen mask on.

Children who have heart surgery are required to stay in the CCU until they have their first urination and bowel movement and are able to eat and drink several meals, starting with liquids and then progressing to solids over the course of a few days. They can then move into a room on the cardiac care floor.

The CCU Lauren is in is cramped—in fact, I question whether they are over capacity. There is not much room between patient beds. The child in the bed next to Lauren can't be more than two feet away. We are separated from her and her visitors by nothing more than a flimsy curtain. There is zero privacy. Other than not actually seeing the patient and her family next to us, we can hear every word and sound that they make. I worry about the risk of any type of germ spreading with such close quarters; especially since all of the children in this unit are so vulnerable post-op. It adds another layer of stress to an already tense situation. I'm sure that this is not the ideal situation for a healing experience. We make the best of it, though, by soothing Lauren with her music player and reading her favorite books close to her ear. As always, we'll do WIT to help our baby girl get healthy and out of here. I can't believe that we actually look forward to the move to a semi-private room.

We both stay with Lauren until late that day. She is drowsy but happy that we are with her. After she falls asleep for the night and seems stable, we drive home to try to get some sleep ourselves before starting the whole process over again tomorrow.

After day three following her surgery, Lauren is urinating and having bowel movements and eating, so she is moved to a room on the cardiac care floor. She seems to be coming around and recovering. She requires less pain medication, is more alert, and is speaking and eating. But when I walk in on the sixth morning, I find a new, young nurse on duty who seems more concerned with making plans for her coffee break than with caring for my daughter. She barely acknowledges me when I enter the room.

After she leaves, I comb Lauren's hair and freshen her up a bit. Her body feels warm. *Does she have a temperature?*

It's bothered me these past few days that Lauren's wounds are not dressed and protected from infection. She is simply wearing a skimpy hospital gown and a pull-up diaper. And while I'm no expert, her wounds do not look good. Between that and her apparent fever, I'm worried. In fact, the day prior, Lauren's new roommate's parents expressed their concerns about why her chest was not covered with sterile dressings.

The young nurse comes back, and I ask her to take Lauren's temperature. She has a fever.

"Didn't you notice that she was warm when you came in this morning?" I demand. "I noticed her temperature as soon as I touched her. I think that you need to make her doctor aware of this, immediately." I am livid but also worried, and with Jim at work, I'm on my own.

The doctor comes relatively quickly, and after looking Lauren over, he decides to do a chest x-ray and a blood test. He wheels her out of the room. I dash to call Jim and ask him to get here as soon as he can. After all the medical missteps we've witnessed over the past two years, I have sensitive antennae for trouble. *Something is happening.*

I hang up and cry, though what I really feel like doing is screaming, and frantic thoughts whirl through my mind:

Why in the world were her chest wounds—her entire chest, for that matter—not covered up with sterile bandages or dressings?

Did she contract an infection in that cramped cardiac care unit?

What if that fever is the sign of an infection?

Why didn't I question the nurses about this?

What does this mean for my child?

The implications are not good. Fever is often an indication of infection, and an infection in a deep chest wound surrounding the heart is quite serious. I am furious with the hospital—and with myself for not questioning their methods sooner. Two nights ago, Jim's parents came to visit, and since Lauren had been improving steadily for five days, they invited us to get dinner and celebrate. My maternal instincts were kicking in—I didn't feel as confident about her recovery as I would like—but I reluctantly left the hospital earlier than usual that night to go with them.

At dinner, Jim's parents cheered Lauren's recovery. But I was hesitant. I did not want to talk about how she was progressing. *Not yet*, I told myself. *I don't want to jinx this. Until they tell us that she is well enough to be discharged, I am not going to celebrate.* I was too worried to enjoy the meal or their company.

Now it seems my fears were well founded. This morning, when I return to the hospital, Dr. Rollins looks grim.

"I suspect an infection is present in or near Lauren's chest wound," he says. "We'll need to take Lauren back down to surgery immediately."

I fight back nausea as he explains that they will need to reopen her chest to examine her wound and to determine where the infection is and what type it is. I am glad that they are acting quickly; we should have some news about what they find by early afternoon. But I'm also enraged and terrified. *This shouldn't be happening*, I rage silently. *They should have taken better care of her.* I know this is going to be a nasty fight: Lauren versus the infection that is now raging in her weakened body.

After the procedure, Lauren is back in the CCU for a day of watchful care and recovery. I question now why she was released to the "cardiac floor" so soon after her initial surgery. Why, with her Down syndrome and weaker immune system, was she not monitored more carefully? I think about that ditzy nurse who didn't even know that Lauren had a fever. I file a formal complaint about her.

We are told that because of the infection, Lauren's deep chest wound won't be resewn shut. It will instead be "packed" in a special manner and her chest will be temporarily wired closed. They do not want to risk masking the infection or allowing it to spread while buried deep inside a closed wound, nor do they want to subject her to more surgery to open and then close the wound. She will receive heavy-duty antibiotics and will be monitored each day with a chest x-ray and blood work. Her doctors insert a port into her chest, giving them easier and less painful access to her tiny veins so they can circulate the medications needed to fight the infection.

After these procedures, Lauren is sent to the ICU for recovery. This has advantages and disadvantages. The plus is that she is monitored more carefully in the ICU, the ICU nurses are more skilled, and there is more room between beds than in the cramped CCU. The minus is little privacy or peace. As in the NICU, the lights are always bright, the unit is a whirlwind of constant activity and noise, and there are a lot of very sick children, many of whom are dying of cancer or suffering from other severe ailments. It is a disturbing, depressing place. There have already been two deaths since Lauren arrived.

They're containing the infection so far, but the medications give Lauren terrible diarrhea, and she is losing weight. We try to help by bringing her yogurt with a high count of "good bacteria" to aid her digestive system. We feed her ice cream for the calories and enjoyable taste. She is always sedated and is usually drowsy. She hardly speaks. But as usual, her spirits are good, and we do our best to always be cheerful around her. We hide as best we can the fact that we are deeply frightened by the physical toll this infection is taking.

On Lauren's third day in the ICU, we talk to another couple we see at the opposite end of the unit. They tell us that their daughter was born with the same heart defect as Lauren, though she does not have Down syndrome.

"Why is she here now?" I ask.

"She has a staph infection in her surgical wound," the mom says.

"Lauren's here with an infection, too," I say.

"Well you know, the CCU has been temporarily shut down," she says. "They quarantined it because of a staph infection outbreak; several children got staph before they realized what was happening."

I'm shocked by this news. *How did they find out all of this while we knew nothing?*

"Excuse me," a nurse says, interrupting our conversation. "I need to speak with you for a moment." The couple walks away to find out what she wants.

I get the impression that the staff does not want us comparing notes. I have a distinct sense that the top priority with this situation is "damage control"—avoiding legal liability. It's probably not a coincidence that they have positioned us as far apart from this other family as possible in the ICU.

When Lauren falls asleep, I walk down to the CCU. It is dark and devoid of patients—a big change from ten days ago, when every bed was full. We were packed like sardines; maybe that's why the staph spread so readily. *When Lauren recovers from this ordeal, I decide, I will file a complaint.* For now, I will say nothing. I don't want to risk compromising her care.

I briefly consider transferring her to Children's Hospital, but I worry that she is not stable enough. I start questioning my decisions. *Maybe we should not have ever come back to this old, unkempt hospital for her follow-up surgery, I think. Maybe we should have started fresh with Children's Hospital.* I am beating myself up with guilt. I thought that Lauren might be better served here because this hospital knows her condition, and their cardiology team has been following her case since her birth. But now doubts gnaw at me.

The trip to Holland is on the verge of becoming a trip to hell. What were the odds that the both of us would end up with serious, life-threatening infections after going under the knife, and in the space of less than a year? Who could have ever predicted this?

Downward Spiral

The next day, we have a consultation with a member of Dr. Rollins's team, and he delivers bad news: the infection is spreading beyond Lauren's wound; they will need to be even more aggressive with the antibiotics and treatment. It is going to be a longer battle than they or we had realized.

I burst into tears at the prospect of all this. The thoughts of Lauren's body being attacked and consumed by this infection make me ill. I almost vomit right in the doctor's office.

Due to the heavy antibiotics and pain medication, Lauren is beginning a slow decline into drowsiness and lethargy. This is the last day that Lauren is cognizant and alert. It is painful for us to see her this way and to watch her physical and mental decline. As each day passes, the nasty infection takes over more of her weak little body. Her kidneys fail, and she has to be catheterized so she can urinate. She is fed intravenously because she can't hold down any food or liquids. Initially, she wore oxygen tubes in her nose, but she is now on a respirator because her lungs have failed. The infection is spreading and ravaging her little body.

Despite all this, each day we arrive optimistic and hopeful for a positive change. We beg for a miracle. I think back on some of the angel moments of our past, and I beseech God to send one again and rescue Lauren before it is too late.

In retrospect, we were in a fog. After weeks of being emotionally worked over—I sometimes feel like we're a couple of overmatched boxers—we can't think straight. We are blind to how far gone

Lauren is. And not one person on her medical team has come right out to tell us how deadly the infection has grown. We do not yet grasp that our baby girl is going to die.

It is Lauren's third birthday week—six weeks have passed since her surgery—and the situation has worsened. Lauren is unconscious now, kept alive only by a respirator and a heart pump. Throughout these nightmare weeks, I have sat by her bedside daily, playing songs on her tape recorder, reading her stories, talking to her, massaging her arms and legs, and caressing her face and hands. Her body is motionless, but I know she hears me and understands that I am there with her. I tell her that it is her birthday and sing the birthday song to her all week. I am praying that God will have mercy—that he will give her strength back as a birthday gift. I am hoping for a miracle.

Meanwhile, baby James, who is now four months old, has been left home alone quite a bit with hired nannies as we keep our watch over Lauren. The guilt that I feel about this only exacerbates my maternal remorse and heartbreak. I can't help but torture myself with guilt and what-if scenarios. I wonder how we got to this point. What could I have done to prevent this? Have her doctors done all that they could? At our weekly meetings with the cardiac and infectious disease teams, they seem to be doing everything possible, using more and more powerful antibiotics, but the harsh reality is that hospitals are breeding grounds for drug-resistant staph, and it is often fatal even for strong, healthy adults. My precious little girl doesn't stand a chance.

I struggle with my desire to go toe to toe with the hospital on this, to accuse them of negligence and threaten to bring in a legal team. Part of me recognizes that I want someone to blame for what is happening to my child, but the logic seems undeniable: for two babies to get the same infection within the same time period, after being kept in the same area of the hospital, indicates to me that the OR or CCU (or both) were contaminated. I do not want to get into a finger-pointing confrontation with my doctors while they are caring for Lauren. I do not want my antagonism to distract them from her care. But as I sit and look at the wreckage of my baby's body, I cannot help but rage. I spend a good amount of each day away from her bed, in the ladies' room, wracked with sobs and sickness.

I have always thought that there is something extraordinary about Lauren, and I firmly believe that she is a child who could prove a miracle. I am not giving up on my baby without a fight.

From a visiting priest, I found out about a local society dedicated to an Italian priest, Padre Pio, whom local believers are looking to have canonized as a saint. In the Catholic Church, a very specific process must play out for someone to become a saint. Part of this process is that the candidate must have at least three miracles proven to have occurred because of his or her intercession. With Padre Pio, one miracle has already been documented and accepted. I intend Lauren to be his second.

One morning, after my meeting with the priest, I drive thirty minutes from my hometown to pick up a Mr. Bello, the head of the local Padre Pio society. He possesses a prized relic of Padre Pio's: his glove.

On the ride back to the hospital, Mr. Bello and I talk about Padre Pio and how sure I am that Lauren will be his second miracle. I feel a kindred spirit with both Mr. Bello and the deceased priest, Padre Pio, because we are all of Italian descent. In fact, Padre Pio's hometown in Italy is located near my ancestors' town and distant family who still reside there. Mr. Bello and I are both hopeful and searching for a miracle—I for my daughter to recover and live and he for the padre to intervene and grant that miracle for his canonization. I proudly tell him about Lauren and what a trooper she has been during her three short years. How pleasant and happy she is despite her very difficult start in life. How I feel special to have been chosen to be her mother. How Lauren has unknowingly taught me poignant lessons about life and love. And how I am now justifying all of our past pain together because we will be the chosen ones to be granted this miracle. "I believe in the power of miracles and prayer, Mr. Bello. We have already experienced some angel moments, as I call them, in the past. I am confident that my hearing about you and the padre are another example of a miraculous intervention."

"Well, Mrs. Barker, these miracles have to happen to someone, so let's hope that this is indeed our lucky day today. Lauren's story of recovery from such a serious and fatal hospital accident would be especially endearing."

We go straight to the ICU when we arrive. Mr. Bello, the visiting priest, another parent of a child in the room, and I all pray over Lauren's comatose body with the padre's glove on her chest. I also hold her hands, once again trying to channel my energy to her to give her the strength to fight. Nothing happens immediately, but I am optimistic that a miracle may occur and Lauren will wake up.

I drive Mr. Bello home, and I pray all the way back to the hospital that I will be greeted with some extraordinary news. But I am disappointed: there is no change. No miracles will occur today.

After the failure of my Padre Pio miracle, I remember another mystical person I've heard about. A few months ago, a friend told me about an astrologer she consulted who was so accurate with his information and predictions for specific circumstances in her life that she was able to overcome all the obstacles in her way and have tremendous success. As soon as I obtain his name and number, I call him. When I explain the urgency and severity of our situation with Lauren, he agrees to see Jim and me immediately. We make an appointment for the next evening, after our hospital visit.

KB Mann is not a psychic. He was a homeopathic physician in his native India, and he is also a trained astrologer, someone who reads a person's astrological chart based on the date and time of their birth. At our meeting, I quickly summarize our past and present situations. He understands that we are desperate. We need to know if Lauren will survive or if there is some way for us to save her.

Gently, he explains that based on my and Lauren's charts, I was "marked" to have a special needs child. And Lauren's chart, he says, indicates that her life will be short. It is likely that she will not survive this terrible ordeal.

"But never say never," he says. "Love is immensely strong, and this can change fate." He gives me a few semiprecious stones to tape to Lauren's body at specific blood-flow points, and explains that these might be able to effect some change. It's worth a try.

We bid him good-bye and promise to keep in touch. Perhaps we're grasping at straws, but when your child is dying, that's what you do. At the very least, Jim and I both appreciate KB's gentle, pragmatic advice.

We don't say it out loud, but Jim and I both know that Lauren is not going to recover. Today, when Jim arrives at the hospital, he asks me to go outside the ICU to talk. There, he gently tells me the medical staff has indicated that there is nothing else that they can do for Lauren.

I cry, but the news is not a surprise. As much as we have been in a fog these past seven weeks, it is evident to both of us that Lauren is gone. I'm a little furious that the staff didn't have the courage to tell me this news to my face—that they told Jim privately and expected him to deliver the news to me—but I can't think about that right now.

"I can't bear to pull her plug," I say. "I feel that I am giving up on my baby. She is still alive."

"Lauren isn't really alive, Liz," Jim says. "Her body is being kept alive by the heart and lung machines. The Lauren we know is gone."

I know he's right, but it is all too much to bear for the moment. I cannot make the decision yet to take my child off life support. "Not tonight," I manage to say.

Jim nods. "Not tonight."

We go back in to hug and say good night to Lauren. All I want to do is go home and crawl into my bed—to hug and rock James. He is now almost five months old, and we have yet to christen him. We have not had the time or energy. And now, if Lauren dies—*when* Lauren dies—I can't imagine mustering the desire for any sort of celebration.

I finally completely lose it on the drive home. I fill the car with tears and screams.

"How could things have gone so terribly wrong for us?" I wail. "It's not fair! Why would God allow such a good little girl like Lauren to be tortured this way after all she has already suffered? Lauren was always so cheerful despite her past pains. It's not fair to baby James either that he is left alone all day long. And that hospital, Jim—it's their fault that Lauren got that staph infection. They'll never admit to having to close down the CCU because of contamination, but I know that they're hiding something from us. I know things didn't have to happen this way."

My grief is turning into fury. Jim tries to comfort me, but I am beyond comfort.

Thankfully, my mood softens the moment that we arrive home and I see and hold baby James. I hug him more fiercely than usual and rock him to sleep in my arms. After he falls asleep, I cry again as I think of my baby girl, all alone and so sick. I wish that she could be in my arms, too.

When I go to bed, I lie there and think, *Maybe I will wake up and find that this was all just a bad nightmare like something from* The Twilight Zone. *Maybe I have been so exhausted and stressed out these past few months that I was delirious, and I will snap out of it, wake up, and Lauren will be okay.* I cry myself to sleep like a baby.

When I wake up the next morning, I realize that I am indeed living the nightmare. My reality is horrid. Today, Jim and I will be asked to do something no parent should ever have to do: approve the removal of life support from our beloved daughter.

She will be heavily sedated with morphine so that she will stop breathing and slip away painlessly, we are assured. This doesn't make us feel better. But we know that if we do not do this now, she will still die, but perhaps in a more traumatic manner. We have no way of knowing if she has any awareness at this point, but I don't want her traumatized if she does. I wonder what she has been thinking (or if she has been thinking) during these past few weeks, and what she will be thinking when this all transpires. Is she sad? Does she know how much we love her? Will she feel fear as she slips away, or a sense of love and peace? I believe that she does know that I have been there with her faithfully, but I keep thinking we should have gotten her away from this terrible hospital, and the guilt I feel over failing to do so is crushing.

Reluctantly, tearfully, we agree to take Lauren off life support. We call with our decision and let them know we will be there soon. Jim drives ahead to the hospital with his dad to speak with the doctors. I will follow in another car with his brother Jeff and his mother. My parents will drive themselves and meet us there with Debby, Lauren's godmother.

It is a somber ride through the Badlands. I am glad that this will be my last ride ever to this wretched place. *I will never set foot in here again after this horrible day,* I promise myself.

When we arrive, Jim and his Dad are red-eyed. All of the medical equipment has been removed from Lauren's body. There is no tape on her face holding the oxygen mask. There are no more IVs. There are no soiled bandages. Her little face is clear and clean. Her hair is smoothed down. She is swaddled like a newborn in a fresh white sheet. Though she is in a deep sleep and completely limp, we lift her out of the hospital bed and hold her. We sit in a semicircle in her room. We are all crying as we pass her body from one to another for final hugs and good-byes. It is alarming that her body is so heavy and bloated. Her nurse explains that this is the result of pounds of fluid built up because her heart and other organs were not functioning.

Jim holds her first. Then she is passed to me. I hug her tightly and kiss her forehead. There is so much that I want to say to her, but my thoughts and feelings are too private to share with all the others around.

"I love you so much," I tell her. I also want to explain why we brought her here, that she needed surgery in order to live. I want to tell her how sorry we are that this went so badly and that she has suffered so much. But all I can do is say "I love you," and pray that she can sense me cradling her.

After we have all had a chance to hold Lauren, she is returned to my arms. Somehow, I know when the life has passed from her body. I burst into fresh tears. I hope that she can read my mind as her spirit leaves her body so she will know my love for her. After a few minutes, the nurse comes in to put Lauren back into bed and to console us. She asks us if she can help pack up Lauren's belongings. I don't answer; I just take my child's things and walk out of the room.

Now that this nightmare is over, I don't want to be pleasant anymore. These people are responsible for Lauren's long, painful death. Out of respect for the other people in the ICU, I don't verbalize what I'm thinking, but inside I am screaming and cursing everyone and everything about this wretched place.

I am overcome with rage; I can't wait to get the hell out of here. I will investigate how this all went so terribly wrong soon, but for now, I just want to run as fast as I can and never look back.

Read in the Stars

As Jim and I walk out of the hospital, alone, a strange, shuddering chill strikes me. I shiver so badly that Jim has to hug me. I have read that when spirits visit they bring cold air with them. I wonder aloud to Jim if this is Lauren's spirit following us out of this doomsday place. Perhaps Lauren is joining us in a group hug. If it is her, I hope that she will find comfort as she passes through whatever happens when a person dies.

"What happens when a body dies?" I wonder aloud. "Where does the soul or spirit go? Does it linger—and if so, for how long?"

Jim has no answers for me.

We decide that Lauren will not be buried in some far-off graveyard. We are going to have her cremated and keep her ashes in a beautiful container that will always remain a part of our family. I will choose a lovely container that can sit on our mantel as a constant reminder of Lauren. It will be a comfort that she is still in our presence in some way. We will have to plan for a funeral, but for now our plan is to crawl into our bed and cry. Jim's parents will take James for the day. We are more spent than we have ever been.

Though it is only lunchtime when we arrive home, we crawl into bed right away. We cry and clutch each other for comfort and fall asleep for hours. The pent-up fatigue of these past seven weeks has caught up to us.

The next two days are a blur of preparation: preparing a memorial booklet for Lauren, choosing songs and readings for the Mass, and writing a heartfelt eulogy from Jim and me that someone else will read. We also gather some of our favorite photos of Lauren to share.

It is amazing and comforting how everyone has pitched in to help us, and we need it. With our parents encouragement, we plan the perfunctory catered buffet at our home afterward for out-of-town relatives. It seems like everyone is doing something. Even our neighbor across the street, Mary Ann, has offered to mind James while we are at the viewing and the funeral Mass. It is best not have him there; we will all be in tears, and it will only frighten him.

At the church, before everyone else arrives for the viewing, Jim and I have final private time with Lauren. I am perturbed because we have to do this with a closed casket. The undertaker told us that this is necessary because of the ravages of the infection on her body. Still, I yearn to see and kiss my baby girl's face, to hug her and hold her as best as I can. I am tempted to ignore him and to defiantly lift the casket lid. But Jim stops me and says that it is best if we remember Lauren as she was and to not have our tender memories tainted with a potentially devastating final image of her illness. I reluctantly back off. Instead, I speak softly to her through the closed lid but with my hands massaging the top of it.

Speaking to Lauren now is not the same as when we were at the hospital. I know that this is just a body now. But I hope that Lauren's spirit is still with us and has not yet moved on to whatever comes next.

As the viewing begins, people stream into the church and up to the front for our receiving line. Their touches strengthen me. I am truly amazed at the tremendous amount of positive energy I am receiving, and at how many people have come to support us. The receiving line stretches down the aisle, out the door, and down the steps of the church and snakes around onto the pavement. Beyond family members and close friends, we see coworkers, staff from the Arc Alliance and KenCrest, and even some of the nurses from William Penn Memorial. *So many people,* I think, astonished at how many lives our daughter has touched. Afterward, we discover how generous these people were, too. We had requested that in lieu of flowers, that people make donations to the nonprofits that were the lifelines to us and to Lauren. We were amazed by the response. Their presence, warmth, and thoughtfulness are what carried us through that difficult day and in the painful months that followed.

And then, it's over. The three days from Lauren's death on April 29 to her funeral on May 2 have been a blur. Now, the day after the funeral, I experience an emotional and physical hangover. I also feel, however, as if a giant weight has been lifted. Although I am very sad, I am feeling something that ambushes me: relief. I am glad that this long and painful ordeal is over. Jim and I have endured nonstop stress since last fall, when we were told that Lauren would need surgery within a few months. And these last two months, helplessly watching as Lauren suffered day after day, have been pure hell. Finally, she is at peace.

So many thoughts go through my head. I smile at the love that surrounded us yesterday. I feel frustration and anger as I try to make sense of what happened and why. I feel guilt over experiencing relief that the horror has finally passed. I feel warmth at the memories of the wonderful times that we had during the two-year period when Lauren was at home and healthy.

I decide that for the next few days, I will stay at home, recuperate, and spend quality time with James. He is now almost five months old, cute as a button, and still looks just like his dad. We call him "mini Jim." He has grown nicely these past two months. And he is sweet natured like Lauren. Although he is an infant, he seems to sense my sadness. When I pick him up to hug him, he digs in with his arms and legs. He does this every time I hold him. Perhaps he has missed me these past two months, but it feels like he's trying to cheer me up. I realize how simple and delightful it is to care for a healthy baby. What a difference not having to worry about a health problem that might crop up at a moment's notice. I bathe, feed, dress, and handle James without worrying that I might do something wrong.

We spend some time in Lauren's room playing with her things. I'm glad I took lots of photos of James and Lauren during the short time they were both at home together. James will not remember anything about his sister, but I will always have these pictures of them, and I will share them with him one day.

For now, I don't change anything in Lauren's room. Everything will stay just as it was the last day she was at home. Our home is filled with reminders and mementos of her. There are her school art projects hanging on my refrigerator and my kitchen desk bulletin board. There are her toys in the den. There is the double stroller that we used to wheel both children, she in the front and James in the back. I won't wash the clothes that Lauren wore on the day she went into the hospital because they have her scent on them. I hang that outfit in her closet with her other clothes and caress them as if she were still in them. I hug her favorite dolls and toys as she would. I look longingly each morning at her Playskool kitchen and recall how she would mimic me making the morning coffee and then serve me a cup of "pretend" coffee. While James sleeps each afternoon, I let my mind run freely over these memories. I wonder if this pain will ever diminish. I don't want to forget Lauren or our memories; I just want not to be so sad. Baby James helps with his big hugs and warm happiness, but the ache is still there.

After that first week, I begin to come back to life. I dread running into acquaintances who may not know of Lauren's death, but I know I need to get out into the world. So James and I venture out—food shopping, visiting family and friends, and taking walks in the neighborhood. However, I am too emotionally raw to return to the demands of my job just yet. I inform my office that I won't be back to work until September, and, as before, they are understanding and supportive. I am continually amazed by their flexibility and kindness. I don't know how we would have managed without it.

I dread Mother's Day as it approaches. Only two weeks have passed since Lauren's death, and I'm in no mood to celebrate. Our families push for us to gather with them for the holiday, but Jim and I elect to take a long car ride to the beach that day, just the three of us, instead. We will pack a lunch and return home for dinner. I can't bear to feign happiness in a crowd so soon, even among those who love us. They have no idea of how brokenhearted we are and the enduring pain we feel from our loss. One month later, on Father's Day, we christen James when he is six months old. I go through the motions of the preparations, but my heart is still heavy with grief. We make it a small, simple party with just family and a couple of close friends. And although the day is lovely, and we are all outside at our home enjoying the weather, children, fun, and food, there is a palpable tinge of sadness to the event. There is happiness and love, but we lack the exuberance of a true celebration. We are all missing Lauren, who should be here with her brother for his special day.

After his christening and for the two months that follow, I relish my time at home with baby James. There are no events to plan or attend. The warm weather and the sunshine help combat my sadness. My youngest sister, Rose, has her second child, Rosie, over Memorial Day weekend, and I spend a good amount of time with her and our children during the week. I also reach out to close friends and other family who have young children and get together with them for playdates. It is comforting when they share their fond memories of Lauren.

Jim and I spend most weekends with his family and their children at his brother's remote mountain lake house, two hours away. It is relaxing and refreshing to go up there, so peaceful to grill dinner and sit out on the deck, under the stars. Each evening brings cool breezes that lull us to sleep. This is exactly the type of subdued and close-knit social activity that Jim and I need for now. We look forward to this escape each weekend.

Fortunately, our summer of sadness passes quickly, and the time off allows me to heal enough emotionally to return to work part-time. Because I am working only three days a week, my income is considerably lower than it was at my peak, but we can manage. We accounted for my lower income when we planned the move to our new home. And, of course, I've been able to retain my great health insurance.

The most difficult part of returning to work is talking about the reason for my absence with my clients. It forces me to rehash the nightmarish recent past more times than I want to. But at the same time, I am grateful that people care enough to ask.

As much as the summer was a healing time for me, not a day goes by that I do not cry for Lauren. On some mornings, waking up from a dream about her will set me off. Other times, seeing some of her photos or possessions brings back a memory that's unbearable. Talking with someone about her, or simply walking into her bedroom—as I do each evening after putting James to bed—starts the tears flowing.

I decide to go back and see my astrologer friend, KB Mann. I bring along my cousin Marie for companionship and because she wants to have a reading from KB, too. I hope that he might offer me pearls of wisdom to help with my grief. I don't know if he is aware that Lauren has died, but I can't imagine he'll be surprised at the news—he knew her grim condition on the evening when we last met. What I really want to do is ask him about my prospects for having more children in the near future. After all that we have seen in the special needs programs and the hospitals, I worry about the well-being of any future children I might have. I also want to ask about my and Jim's futures regarding our jobs and health. We have endured so much stress that I harbor vague worry about both of us. And I want to ask if he has any indication that Lauren's spirit is at peace. Perhaps I am just yearning for some upbeat news to counter my persistent sadness.

When we sit down together, KB admits that he saw little hope for Lauren on that desperate evening when we first met, but he gave me the crystals in the hope they would offer some measure of help.

"If Lauren had lived, she may have suffered more," he says. "Her death was a blessing."

If he's right, then her death was indeed a blessing for us both, because her suffering would have been my suffering; he knows the deep bond that we shared.

"Her birth chart clearly shows that her life was to be a short and difficult one," he says.

There's an inevitability to this that comforts me. Perhaps Lauren was only meant to be with me for a short time. But why?

KB answers my unspoken question immediately. He says that the fact that I have been so profoundly touched and changed by my experience with Lauren is also revealed in my chart. "There is a reason for this," he explains. "You now have seen another paradigm of life. You have experienced and survived the unintended and the unexpected."

He sees my confusion, so he goes on: "What seem to be tragedies that happened to you are really life lessons learned. When the time is right, I predict that you will share these precious gifts with others. In the future, when you are ready, I see you as a speaker in the public eye, inspiring and helping others. Because this will be a joy for you to share, you will be highly successful. And as a result of your success, you will be a philanthropist. During this period of your life, you will be at your summit with peace, happiness, and security. You have learned many life lessons in a harsh manner, yet survived. And you will thrive. You will be a mentor to others, Liz."

I'm dumbstruck for a moment. "Wow, KB, that's quite a prophecy!" I finally say.

What he says about Lauren is a comfort to me, but the rest of it seems cryptic. I think of a philanthropist as someone who is extremely wealthy and gives money to charitable causes.

"Jim and I do okay financially, and we enjoy helping those in need, but we're not wealthy," I say. "It's hard for me to imagine us as 'philanthropists.' How in the world am I going to become that?"

"You'll see," KB says, giving me a sly grin. "I can't tell you the specifics, as it may alter the course of your life. You will just have to be open and ready when these opportunities come along."

Okay. This is good news, I think.

He then tells me it's likely that Lauren's spirit will be reborn because she was so young and pure. "To compensate for her suffering in this life, her next life will be completely different and better than this past one," he says. "It will be filled with happiness and greatness. Lauren left this world with good karma, and her spirit knew that it was her destiny to have a short life. She is at peace."

I'm not sure how much of this I really believe, but it is a comfort when he tells me that she knew how deeply we all loved her and that what happened was not our fault.

"When people are reborn," I ask, "how does it work? Will she be reborn into our family?"

"That's uncertain," he says. "Reincarnation works in different ways for different people."

I ask my most pressing question: "I'd like to get pregnant again soon so that James will have at least one sibling," I say. "What do you see in my chart about that? Will my next child be healthy?"

KB's mood changes dramatically, from upbeat to somber, with this query. "You will have reproductive problems," he says flatly. He reviews my chart and advises me that the best time for me to have another child is in 1997—eight years from now.

"By then I'll be forty," I say. Surely he knows that the older an expectant mother is, the greater her risk of having a child with Down syndrome, right? Although we loved Lauren with all our hearts, I do not want to ride that emotional roller coaster again. I could not bear to see another baby go through the pain and trauma that she did. And it's not just Down syndrome I'm worried about; all types of risks for childbirth increase dramatically as a woman ages.

I ask him to be more specific about the "reproductive problems" he's referencing, but he will not elaborate, not wanting to manipulate the future. He simply repeats his advice: "Do not become pregnant for some time," he says sternly.

He must know that I probably won't heed his advice. I have my own plans, and while I trust much of what he has told me, I can't accept that I should wait eight years before having another child. *Maybe he's worried about me having another ectopic pregnancy or another child with a genetic defect,* I think, *but I can handle that. Whatever happens, happens. I'll deal with it as it comes.* I waited long enough to begin my family, and now, at age thirty-three, after losing my Lauren, I desperately want more children.

I sincerely thank KB for his time and his insights and leave. In my mind, I have already dismissed his warnings.

Little do I know that he's a better predictor of the future than I could ever imagine.

The C Word

On the drive home, I can't stop thinking about KB's predictions. I share them with Marie, who is still astonished by what he told her about her life. I think about his reassuring words about Lauren and how all of this played out, and it comforts me to know that she understood her destiny and knew we loved her. But the philanthropist thing is so strange. *I don't expect to come into a fortune or inheritance, or to hit Powerball, any time in the near future,* I think. The whole idea feels a bit ridiculous to me. I decide to ignore that part of KB's predictions and move forward with my own plans.

Time seems to pass quickly as one holiday follows another: Halloween, Thanksgiving, James's first birthday, and then Christmas. Celebrating with little James and creating new memories with him is a pleasure, but it is sad for me, too; I can't help but reflect on the holidays we shared with Lauren not so long ago. But I do my best to balance the two—the nostalgia (which, I learn, literally means "pain of remembering") with the joy.

James is a sweet baby. I am thankful each day for his health, his growth and development, and the love and healing that he brings to us. We have been practicing his walking with him. Jim and I sit on the floor about eight feet from each other and hold out our arms to either send or to receive him as he tries his wobbly walk between us. We do this the morning of his birthday and are delighted to see him walk the entire length on his own for the first time. What a great birthday present! We videotape him as he decides to do this several times over, encouraged by our clapping. It's a great day for our son alone; there are no memories of Lauren present to haunt us.

Christmas, however, which comes one week later, is painful. I can't stop thinking about our last Christmas, which was nearly perfect: toddler Lauren tearing through all of her gifts, newborn baby James sitting in my lap and taking it all in with his big brown eyes. Last year on Christmas morning, we felt blessed to be sharing the magic of the holiday with two little ones. This year, as I put James on the floor in front of the tree, my throat closes with a rush of mixed emotions. I delight in his happiness at the wonder of the tree, and his excitement as I help him tear open the paper, but I can't stop thinking about Lauren as she was, just one year ago.

Why does this still cause me so much anguish? Jim hasn't seemed upset around any of the holidays we've celebrated this year without Lauren. Does he not have the same emotional attachments that I do, or is he simply better at blocking them out? I can't figure it out, but I am glad for his strength. Our lives would be a mess if we were both upset and teary eyed all the time.

We have had many discussions about the past four years in the months since Lauren passed. During one conversation, Jim asks, "What could be worse than losing your child?"

I don't know what prompts me to say it, but I blurt out, "Well, one of us could become terminally ill and the survivor would be left to raise our child alone."

Saying this out loud seems a bit risky—like I'm tempting fate—but the truth is, I figure the universe has probably had enough of pummeling us at this point. *With all we've been through,* I think, *we are owed at least fifty years of peace and quiet.*

When my birthday rolls around in January, we decide that it might be refreshing for the two of us to have a change of scenery to celebrate and to ward off sad memories. It would also be nice to get away from the bitter Philadelphia winter to a warm place. We are delighted to learn that Annie, who looked after James so well when

Lauren was hospitalized, is available to come back to our home and stay with James.

Jim loves sailing and I love the beach, so we decide that the best medicine for our blues is a four-night trip to the Bitter End Yacht Club in Virgin Gorda, British Virgin Islands. We have never been here before, but the brochures and our travel agent convince us. It is a beautiful tropical resort that can be reached only by boat. If you want to leave the resort to take a tour or visit other restaurants, you have to take a charter boat or a ferry. But we have no ambitions to leave the resort. We want nothing but peace, serenity, beauty, and relaxation.

Our greatest exertion on the trip consists of going on a couple of day tours offered for sailing, snorkeling, and touring natural attractions. It is wonderful to be so relaxed! Each day at happy hour, we visit our favorite beachfront bar and enjoy a potent piña colada made by a friendly bartender named Eddie, then take a short nap before dinner. It's the first time in years that we've been able to truly unwind from our tension, stress, and heartache.

It is a joy to see James when we get home. I missed him every day that we were gone. But I know that I needed this getaway to clear my head and lift my melancholy. I feel energized.

About three weeks after our trip, some of my colleagues invite me to lunch. As we sit at our table and wait for our food, I am overwhelmed by unusual hunger pangs.

It must be PMS, I think. Each month, just before my menstrual period, I become ravenous and eat much more at each meal than I normally do.

But after a few days of this extraordinary hunger, I realize that this is not my usual pattern. And when I realize my period is late, everything clicks into place. *I'm pregnant!* I am giddy with the thought that this might be the case, and I can't wait to find out for sure. When I go food shopping with James on Friday, I pick up a home pregnancy test kit, and I perform the test after lunch, while James is napping.

I wait anxiously for the allotted time to pass. Finally, it's time, and I look at the stick. Two blue lines. "Yeah!" I shout out loud. I immediately call my ob-gyn office and make an appointment to confirm things with a blood test.

Perhaps it was the trip that snapped me out of my nine months of mourning and helped me become pregnant. *Or maybe I became pregnant* during *the trip,* I think, *and the early flood of hormones has triggered a more placid and happy mood.* Whatever the reason, and whenever it actually happened, I am overjoyed at the prospect of having another child.

The next week, after an exam and blood test, my ob-gyn confirms that I am indeed about five weeks pregnant; I did conceive while on that wonderful vacation.

This medical practice has all of my records from my prior pregnancies: my pregnancy and delivery with Lauren, my ectopic pregnancy and surgery, and my excellent, easy pregnancy and delivery with James. I am too embarrassed to tell them about KB's predictions, but I do express concern about my past troubles and inquire if they will see me more frequently because of them.

"Come back in four weeks," my doctor tells me, "and we'll discuss your options then. We'll talk about CVS genetic testing and monitoring your blood work."

One thing is for sure: this pregnancy is not like the ectopic pregnancy that led to my surgery and hepatitis. I do not have any spotting or cramping; I am confident that this is a normal pregnancy. But I won't feel completely secure until we do the CVS test and find out whether the baby is genetically healthy. KB's words of warning continue to worry me.

My CVS genetic test takes place at the prestigious Thomas Jefferson Hospital in Center City Philadelphia during my fifteenth week of pregnancy. I am nervous about the results, and I sense that Jim is, too, though neither one of us says anything. We are wary of what this test may reveal about our unborn baby. And if something abnormal is discovered, how will we decide what to do? The positive thing about the test is that we get to find out the sex of the baby. I am hoping for a girl.

By this point in the pregnancy, especially because it is my third pregnancy, my rounded belly is protruding already. I have had to start wearing maternity clothes. This makes me even more anxious about the test results. *If we find out something is wrong with our child, will it be more difficult to terminate my pregnancy, since everyone knows I'm pregnant?* I wonder. *Could I go through with that, even if it seems necessary?* I want to block these scenarios out and think positively, because I feel great, but KB's words haunt me.

I receive the call from the genetic specialist on my day off.

"Your baby is genetically fine," she says cheerfully. "In fact, he appears to be quite healthy. It looks like he will be a large baby, just like his siblings."

I am a little disappointed that I won't be having another girl but, of course, am hugely relieved that my baby is healthy. I immediately phone Jim with the news. Little James and I celebrate at lunch with a toast of our juice glasses.

"You're going to be a big brother!" I tell him, laughing.

After lunch, when I put him down for his nap, I lie down, too. With the tension and worry about the test gone now, I am ready for a rest. When I wake up an hour later, I feel refreshed. I look forward to a happy weekend of celebrating the good news.

Five days before my twenty-week ultrasound to check on the fetus, I begin to feel ill. I am tired, I am a bit feverish, and I have an odd pain along the side of my right breast. I wore a new bra recently, and I felt that it was chafing me on that side; I kept tugging at it and itching that spot. It was more annoying than anything else. But now that I feel feverish, I worry that something is up. I immediately make a doctor's appointment. At our special needs programs, I saw the detrimental effects fevers or infections during pregnancy can have on a baby. I want to take no chances.

I probe my right breast after I hang up with the receptionist at my doctor's office, and I feel a small lump there that I've never noticed before. I suspect that it is what's causing my discomfort. My cloud of worry grows darker. *This is going to turn out to be something innocent,* I tell myself. But I'm not so sure.

I see the doctor two days later, and he performs a manual examination.

"It feels like a clogged milk duct to me," he says. "Nothing to be concerned about."

He did a breast exam on me just a few weeks ago, when he examined me to confirm my pregnancy, and he did not detect this lump then. He seems pretty confident that it's a milk duct.

"Just to be safe, I'll write a prescription for you to have an ultrasound on your right breast when you come in for your fetal ultrasound next week, okay?" he says. "The ultrasound will give us a better look at this. But I am not worried, it is likely just a side effect of your pregnancy. I'll have the test results the next day and I'll contact you immediately afterward. For now, go home and try not to let it bother you."

Easy for him to say. I am cranky and agitated by the extra weight I'm already carrying, and even with his reassurances, I'm nervous about this lump. *This should be a joyful time,* I think. *Why is this happening to me?*

I arrive at the hospital for my two ultrasound tests to find that the radiology department is running behind schedule. *Of course.* It's my day off from work, and I'm paying for a babysitter for James while I'm here. I immediately sink into a bad mood. I'm not only wasting my precious time off, I'm paying for the privilege. After waiting for more than an hour, I begin to get flashbacks of the many unpleasant times we had when Lauren was hospitalized—all the difficult people and uncaring institutions we encountered—and I grow more and more frustrated.

What's the holdup here? I fume. *I am the only one sitting in this waiting area. Did they all take lunch and forget about me?* As time drags on, my agitation increases further. *Do they think that their time is more valuable than mine?*

Finally, I stand up. "To heck with this," I say out loud. "I'm leaving." I get up and begin to walk out.

Just as I'm storming out, a young woman comes out of a nearby office, seemingly out of the blue. "Where are you headed?" she asks kindly.

With barely controlled anger, I tell her about my wait and how annoyed and uncomfortable I am.

She is extremely sympathetic. "I'm so sorry," she says. "But please, come with me. I can't let you leave like this." She takes me by the arm and leads me back to the ultrasound area. "Just wait one moment, I'll be right back."

She disappears behind a door, and in less than a minute she walks back out with a technician.

"Let's get you to the prep area," the technician says.

I look at the young woman. "Thank you so much," I say, overcome with gratitude.

"You're very welcome," she says. She holds out her hand, and I take it in mine. "I'm Robin Goldstein," she says. "Will you stop by my office before you leave? I'll be in there waiting for you when you're finished here."

"Of course," I say. "And again, thank you for your help."

That this complete stranger has appeared out of nowhere and redeemed my faith in people reminds me of how Jim and I happened upon Mrs. Goodman at Thomas Johnson Hospital a few years back, when we were despondent over the delay of Lauren's trach tube removal. *Another angel moment,* I think.

When the test is over, the technician comes over with a serious expression. "Do not ignore this lump," she says sternly. "The results will be sent to your doctor this afternoon, and I encourage you to call him tomorrow if he doesn't call you." Before leaving, she repeats her warning once more: "Do not ignore this lump."

A chill runs up my spine. I don't know what to say. It is getting late, I am getting hungry, and I still have an hour drive to get home, so I don't dawdle. I stop by Robin's office to thank her and then leave. I think about the technician's words on the way home. Will they have to do some kind of a procedure to unclog this milk duct, or will it be enough to do some therapy with hot compresses? If it's just a clogged duct, why did the technician seem so serious?

My doctor calls in the morning.

"I think you should go to see Dr. Palma at Richland Memorial," he says. "He's a surgeon; he'll be able to do a more thorough examination of the lump."

Dr. Palma has already read my test results when I arrive. He tries to aspirate the lump by putting a needle into it to draw liquid out, but nothing comes out. He doesn't seem upset or surprised by this.

"I'd like you to have this lump removed so that it can be better examined," he says. "It's not a big procedure; it can be done with a local anesthetic on an outpatient basis. Then a pathologist can analyze the lump to see why it formed and why it has been giving you trouble."

"So I'll be awake for the procedure?" I ask. The idea makes me a little nervous.

"Yes," he says, "but the area will be numb—you won't feel anything."

He explains all of this quite matter-of-factly, and he seems competent. I go along with his recommendations. I'm still working under the assumption that we are talking about a clogged gland or duct. I set up the appointment for one week later, on my next day off from work, Friday.

When I get home, I tell my mother, who is there babysitting James, about my conversation with Dr. Palma. She grows a bit upset. She questions me about what they might be looking for.

"Did they say anything about breast cancer?" she asks.

"God, no," I reply. "Why would you even think that? I am only thirty-four, and we have no history of breast cancer—or any cancer—in our family. No, it couldn't be breast cancer, I'm too young . . . and wouldn't one of these doctors have said something about that possibility to me by now?" But KB's words are troubling me now. Could this be the problem that he forecast?

From that day on, I begin to climb a new wall of worry. My happiness over my pregnancy evaporates. I can't wait to get my procedure over with and to find out what the lump is, what caused it, and what can be done about it. I don't dare even think about the other possibility. It would just be too much.

Jim accompanies me on the day of the procedure. They give me an IV sedative to calm my nerves and a set of earbuds through which they play calming music. I can still hear the muffled sound of the doctor and the nurses talking, but the music helps distract me a bit. They give me the numbing medication for the surgery. It is an odd feeling to be awake but not feel pain.

When the procedure's done, they wheel me into the recovery area, and the nurse there gives me instructions about how to care for the small wound that now exists where the lump used to be.

"You'll want to remove these drains after twenty-four hours," she says. "And we'd like you to come back in to see Dr. Palma on Monday morning to go over the biopsy results." Her job done, she discharges me.

"Isn't Dr. Palma going to come in to see me before I leave?" I ask. I expected that he would at least say something to me about what he saw when he went in and what the lump looked like before I went home today.

"Dr. Palma has another procedure on his schedule, so he can't see you now," she says. "But he'll see you on Monday."

I rationalize this to mean that there isn't anything seriously wrong. *If he saw something concerning during the procedure,* I reason, *he would come to speak with me right away.*

Over the weekend, as I speak with more family and friends about my procedure, they all bring up the question of breast cancer. No, I reply. Can't be. I am more concerned, based on the trouble I had nursing James when he was an infant, that there is something wrong with my mammary glands and that I won't be able to breast-feed our new baby. Still, I feel unsettled all weekend.

No one trains doctors on how to break bad news. You won't see a class in compassion or communication skills in any medical school curriculum, despite studies having shown that the state of mind of a patient has a great deal to do with his or her recovery.

On Monday morning, Dr. Palma calls Jim and me into his office.

"How was your weekend?" he asks, and I can tell that he's nervous.

He makes a bit more small talk, and then, after the pleasantries are over, he blurts out in rapid succession, "I have some bad news for you. The lump is cancerous. You have breast cancer. You are going to need to have a mastectomy and then chemotherapy, but first you will have to terminate your pregnancy."

My mind goes blank. I just stare at him.

He continues to talk, but it's just noise to me. I keep sitting there, staring. Then the dam breaks: I begin shrieking and sobbing.

"You have no idea how devastating this is," I tell him. "I just lost my little girl, who was three years old, a year ago. I am still grieving. And now you are asking me to terminate a healthy baby boy?"

"Mrs. Barker, you have to," he replies. "You need to save yourself, and think of your husband and your little boy, who both need you."

He goes on to tell me what will happen. They will inject the fetus with a chemical solution that will kill him. Then I will deliver a dead baby. It is horrifying, and made worse by the vivid memories of all of the medical trauma we went through with Lauren.

"No!" I scream. "I will go insane if I have to do this. We've been through so much already. I can't do this."

No answer from the doctor.

I press further. "This also means that I will never be able to have any more children, doesn't it?"

"Yes, Mrs. Barker, that is likely true, but you can't think about that now," Dr. Palma answers. "You need to focus on saving yourself and doing what I have suggested as soon as possible."

I sit there and cry as his words sink in. I feel betrayed. I wonder if God has turned his back on us. How could all of these terrible things be happening, one after the other? This has been going on relentlessly for four years now: Lauren's Down syndrome and medical complications, my ectopic pregnancy, my hepatitis infection, Lauren's slow, painful death—and now this? What kind of cruel universe is this where a mother, newly pregnant after losing a child, gets breast cancer?

What in God's name did I ever do to deserve all of this? When will it all stop?

The morbid discussion that Jim and I had a few months back, when he asked what could be worse than losing Lauren, comes to mind. We agreed then that one of us dying and the survivor being left to raise James alone would be worse. That scenario is now very much a possibility. I also wonder about KB Mann's prediction. Is this that prophecy coming to pass? If so, I'm sorry that I didn't listen.

I barely hear Dr. Palma's parting words about follow-up and next steps. In the car, my mind is so shaky that I ask Jim to repeat what I have just been told in there so that I can confirm that I heard it all correctly. Jim can barely contain his emotions as he relays the information. We both break down and cry, hugging each other. What words we can manage are disjointed and confused:

"Why in the world are we being punished?"

"We are good people, why is this happening?"

"This is so surreal."

Finally, I scream, "What are we going to do?"

Darned if KB's warning to me about getting pregnant didn't come true! He said I would have "reproductive problems" . . . well, breast cancer diagnosed while very pregnant sure is a reproductive problem, all right. But I didn't heed his warning. It just didn't seem logical at the time.

Now it certainly does. And it is no wonder that I was susceptible to cancer, especially in my breast. I have endured nonstop physical and mental stress since the day Lauren was born, and I've had no physical or mental outlet for it because I've never seemed to be able to find time for a therapist or an exercise program. And the double whammy of my ectopic pregnancy and subsequent hepatitis diagnosis were literally serious body blows. I was stressed all during my pregnancy with James—worried about Lauren's heart catheterization, pre-op preparations, and the need for her massive blood drive—and it didn't get any better after his birth. The worst blow, of course, was having to witness my baby girl's slow and painful death. And now this fourth pregnancy, although very much wanted, feels like it's going to be the last straw—like it may physically break me.

It is evident to me now that I have been beaten up pretty badly in these past five years. I am convinced that the stress of these circumstances compromised my immune system, and that's what opened the doors to cancer setting in. And because I am pregnant and my breasts are literally growing, the cancer found its perfect host site.

Champions

The ten-minute ride home seems like an eternity. My mind is racing: Who will take care of James? How will we handle yet another trauma? What are the implications of breast cancer for a young woman like me? What are the statistics on remission, recurrence, and longevity? All these questions, and I have no answers.

My mother is waiting for us, and she can tell that our news is not good. Her face falls. I slump in a chair as she and Jim talk about the appointment. Jim calls his parents, and they both come over to be with us. My dad comes over as well. Jim's parents suggest that we immediately call their close friend, Dr. Scot Fisher, for advice. Scot has been a radiation oncologist at the prestigious Harrison University Hospital for a dozen years.

My father-in-law dials Scot's office and because it is he who is calling, Scot immediately takes the call. On speaker phone, Jim and his dad explain the situation that has evolved with my pregnancy as well as the doctor's frightening and seemingly rash prognosis and plan of action. Scot dives right in to our situation, bless him.

After hearing what's happened so far, he has a lot to say.

"First of all," he says, "please don't take any action or make any decisions until I make some phone calls to investigate your situation and discuss options with my colleagues."

"Do you think Dr. Palma is wrong about what I should do?" I ask.

"I certainly don't feel that the advice that he gave you was well thought out or researched," he says. "I'm curious: how did you end up going to this local doctor who is not a cancer specialist or even a breast surgeon?"

The second he says it, I realize how strange it is. *Why we didn't immediately make plans to consult with a specialist in this field after getting the news today?* I wonder. But I know why. The answer is, we were too shocked to think straight. We were frightened, and one way to address that fear was to agree to act solely on that doctor's recommendation.

I can't think of too many better examples of the importance of an objective advocate who's not emotionally attached to your health care ups and downs. We're all human; we all suffer from fear, shock, and grief. When we do, we're not rational. We don't think about second opinions and clinical research and other options. Having someone like Scot at hand to lend professional perspective to my situation is already improving my situation.

His advice doesn't change my diagnosis. I still have breast cancer. But it does change our thinking about how to regard this other doctor's quick recommendation for an abortion. Scot is making it clear that it is not necessarily warranted, or the best option. And all his advice makes a great deal of sense. I am comforted and begin to feel optimistic.

"I'm going to prescribe a mild sedative for you to help you remain calm this next couple of days while we're sorting things out," Scot says as our conversation winds to an end. "I'm going to make some calls, and then I'll get back to you with more information—I should have a better grasp on things within a day or two."

Jim and I both feel relieved, at least for now. Both sets of parents, however, do not seem as appeased. They are incredulous about our continuous stretch of misfortune. They have walked with us every step through these nightmarish four years and suffered with us the way only parents can suffer for their children. I hate that we have put them through so much pain. But it is a huge bright spot that we have had them, as well as other family members and good friends, here supporting us. We are lucky to have people in our lives who love and care for us. I know that as this new challenge unfolds, we're going to need to lean on them again.

I sit in my kitchen, attempting to absorb all that has occurred in the past few hours, and I find myself thinking of how we've been lucky enough, to quote Blanche Du Bois, to "rely on the kindness of strangers." It is truly miraculous how many complete strangers have crossed our path at just the right moments, when we were in crisis. These "angels" intervened and carried us through. I think of Mrs. Goodman, who came to our aid when we were so despondent about the delay with Lauren's trach removal. I think of Robin, who stopped me when I was about to walk out of my ultrasound appointment after the long delay. I shudder to think about how much worse my cancer might have become if she had not stopped me on my way out and literally taken me by the arm and walked me to the test area. If it weren't for her, I probably would have left that day without having the ultrasound test done, and the cancer would have continued to fester in my breast, undetected, through the rest of my pregnancy, growing rapidly, until it was widespread or metastasized. Robin, a complete stranger, truly saved my life. And now we have Scot, who is going to intervene on our behalf and will hopefully save our baby boy's life. Small miracles in the midst of fear and trepidation.

Perhaps one day I will be able to help or save someone else, I think as I sit here. *Maybe the purpose of all of this adversity is to teach me how to be a survivor, to make me stronger. Maybe I am supposed to be an example, helping to inspire others to work through the travails of their lives.* And as I think these things, I make a decision: I will do whatever it takes to battle this disease and win. *I want my baby and me to live, and I am going to fight for the two of us. I am tired of being sad and stomped on. I want my life back, and I am going to fight for it!*

As soon as these thoughts come into my head, I remember what KB said: *"You will be in the public eye as a speaker. This work will be the pinnacle of your life and you will inspire others. You will be very successful and fulfilled, and you will enjoy being a philanthropist as a result."*

While I don't know what my immediate future holds, I am energized by this revelation.

Surprisingly, with the aid of the sedative Scot prescribed for me, I fall asleep tonight with no difficulty. But I wake up in the middle of the night in a cold sweat. Sitting upright in bed, all I can think is, *I have cancer. Am I going to die?*

I am committed to this fight, but will my strength be enough? Jim wakes as well and sits up to give me a hug and tells me to get some rest. I sink back onto the bed and fall asleep.

True to his word, Scot calls this morning with excellent news. He has taken the time to consult not only with his colleagues but also with a handful of hospitals and oncology specialists around the country regarding my case. Because breast cancer during pregnancy is rare, there is not a great deal of data about treatment and results. But the consensus is that I should take a more moderate approach than Dr. Palma has recommended. Mastectomies and surgeries have been done on pregnant women with good results.

"The first step I suggest is a mastectomy to see exactly what is left after the removal of the lump," Scot says. "Depending on what the surgery reveals, if the cancer has spread to any lymph nodes, and if so, how many, that information will dictate what needs to follow."

"Have any women undergone chemotherapy while pregnant and delivered healthy babies?" I ask, and I hold my breath, fearful of what his response will be.

"Yes," he says, "especially if the chemo occurs in the latter part of their pregnancy, after the baby has already developed."

I let out the breath I've been holding in. If I do need chemotherapy, it won't be until my third trimester.

"By the time you need chemo—*if* you need it—your baby's vital organs will already have formed and he will mostly be in a growth stage," Scot says. "But we're getting ahead of ourselves. Let's go one step at a time, starting with the mastectomy."

"Okay," I agree. "I don't want to wait. I'm ready to have it as soon as it can be arranged."

"I'll make arrangements for all of the preliminary tests you need and schedule a surgical date with the top surgeon at my hospital as soon as possible," he says. "I think we'll be able to get you in next week."

After I hang up with Scott, my entire family begins to mobilize regarding my job and child care for baby James. My mother calls my boss and explains my circumstances: I will not be coming back to work, at all, for a while. I will need tests before the surgery. Then I will need a good amount of time for recovery. Finally, if the cancer has spread at all, I may need chemotherapy for six months. She promises to keep them updated on my situation and gives them her phone number. Once again, they are unbelievably understanding about my situation and assure me that my clients will be taken care of by the capable assistants there.

By the end of the day, Scot calls to let me know that the pre-surgery tests have been set up. This is the kind of responsiveness that I've been craving for four years: medical professionals who actually seem to care! On Friday, I will undergo an MRI so they can look at my bones for evidence of cancer. They will also perform a thorough ultrasound of my abdominal area—liver, gall bladder, etc.—to see if there are any signs of disease there. X-rays are not recommended for pregnant women, but Scot has clearly ordered the most complete battery of nonradiation tests possible, which should give him a good indication of what stage my cancer has reached or whether it has spread to any other parts of my body.

The next few days are a blur as I prepare both myself and my household for my upcoming absence. I arrange care for James. I shop for groceries to make sure that we have food for James as well as for Jim and me in the days following the procedure. I get my desk in order and tell Jim where our important paperwork—wills, bills, benefits, and life insurance policies—are located. That part is uncomfortable. *I do what I have to do because I must,* I tell myself. There is no other choice. I've already learned this lesson: *What will be, will be.* All I can do now is roll with it and keep positive for an optimum outcome. I can't imagine not making it through surgery or not coming back to the people and home that I love. I will not leave my husband and son alone. I will do whatever it takes to beat this and be there for them.

And I get myself a pair of pajamas that button down the front for easier access to my incision. It's like I'm getting ready for a big vacation—but unfortunately, this won't be a pleasure trip.

Scot calls late on Friday to give me the results of my pre-op tests.

"All of the tests we did came back clean," he says, sounding cheerful. "There does not appear to be any cancer anywhere else in your body."

I send Robin silent thanks for making sure I had that ultrasound that day. I feel like I am going to be okay after all. Now we just need to see what the surgery will reveal. There's still a chance that the cancer might have spread to the lymph nodes in my armpit.

It's Memorial Day weekend, and we spend both days with relatives—Jim's family on Saturday and my family on Sunday for Rosie's second-birthday party. It's a happy occasion, but the atmosphere is subdued because everyone knows that I am going in for surgery the next day. It isn't meant to be, I know, but on both days it feels eerily like a good-bye party. I have to remind myself that the news from my pre-op tests was all positive.

It isn't good-bye, it is a bon voyage for my new journey, I tell myself. *This love and support I am receiving from everyone is my going-away present for my trip to the hospital.*

We have to leave the party early on Sunday evening because I have to be at the hospital by 6:30 a.m. As we depart, my parents, brother, and sisters cry, hug me, and wish me well. I feel their love, and it fills me with hope and strength.

I wake up the morning of my surgery feeling confident and unafraid. Perhaps it is because of all of the positive news Scot gave me. Perhaps it is because of the outpouring of love I experienced over the weekend. Or perhaps it is because after all I have gone through previously, I know I can survive this. I am not afraid. I simply want to get it over with.

Jim's father accompanies us to the hospital to provide Jim emotional support while I'm in surgery. The two of them walk with my gurney up to the OR door; they both have tears in their eyes. They each kiss me on the forehead and say that I am going to do just fine. Then I'm wheeled away. *Here we go.*

Although I am groggy from a preliminary anesthetic, I can feel my eyes widen as we enter the OR. It is huge and cold.

"I've never seen so many pairs of surgical scissors in my life," I say to one of the nurses. It seems like there are hundreds of them lined up on a nearby table. As they prepare to put me under, I pray to Lauren: *Please, be with me and your baby brother in my belly, and help me make it through this operation without incident.* I pray to God: *Please don't let them find cancer anywhere else in my body.*

"Can you count backwards from ten for me?" a nurse asks.

I make it to nine.

I awake in the recovery room to feel a sharp pain in my right breast, like someone is slicing the skin there open. Before I wake fully and understand that I am in recovery, I feel a rush of panic that perhaps I've woken up during the surgery.

"It hurts," I say to the nurse standing by my bed. "Can I have something for the pain?"

"You're not due for more pain medication yet," she says gently, "and if you take more, it might harm your baby."

"Okay," I reply. I will not do anything to jeopardize the health of this baby. I brace myself to deal with the pain until it is time to have another sedative. I remind myself that pain means I'm still alive.

They wheel me out of the surgical suite, and Jim, his dad, and Scot are right there to greet me. Scot has already spoken with my surgeon, Dr. Wolcott, who is the head of surgery at Harrison, and again, the news is pretty encouraging. The lump of cancerous tissue had been relatively contained when Dr. Palma removed it. There was no cancer in the remainder of the breast tissue, which is good.

"Two of the fifteen lymph nodes that Dr. Wolcott removed did have cancer cells in them, however," says Scot, "so I'm afraid you'll need to undergo chemotherapy."

It is not the ideal scenario, but it is nowhere near the worst-case scenario, either. We decide that as soon as I have healed from the surgery, in about three weeks, I will begin a six-month regimen of chemotherapy.

I am fortunate enough to have a private room. Everyone here is nice to me. I can't imagine they've seen many pregnant women recovering from mastectomies, and this elicits sympathy from many of the women on the floor. The five-day stay quickly becomes boring, however. I'm ready to get out of here.

I'm recovering rapidly, but I am filled with anxiety. I do not want to see what is beneath my bandages. The short week before surgery, I had no time to do research into mastectomies; I spent all my time getting tests done and making preparations. Now I am envisioning a right breast that looks like a flattened volcano cone, a crater, or a perhaps a mountain that's been subjected to mountaintop removal mining. Eventually I will have to look, but I am dreading it.

Because I am pregnant, the doctors recommended that I not do the typical dual procedure that many women have done: a mastectomy to remove the cancerous breast and then the immediate construction of a new breast using my abdominal fat or a saline implant. This dual procedure would leave me on the operating room table for several additional hours, and more anesthesia equals more risk, not just to me but also to my unborn baby.

"The goal," my surgeon said, "is to get in and get out as quickly as possible."

I wholeheartedly agreed. *There will be time later to consider my reconstruction options,* I told myself.

Finally, I am discharged. Visiting nurses will come to our home each day for a week to check my wound, my drains, and my progress. They are all quite nice.

One day, a young nurse asks me if I have seen my breast. "No," I reply. "I am too afraid to look at it."

"It doesn't look that bad at all, Mrs. Barker," she says sincerely. I ask her to describe it for me, and she tells me that I do not have a crater or a concave look at all. There is still breast tissue in place, she says, which makes it look like I have a budding preteen-size breast—except that there is no nipple and a long, curved scar underneath.

"I can draw you a picture of it if you like," she says kindly.

"Really?" I say. "I would like that."

She draws it, and when she's done, I take a tentative peek at the image.

"That's it?" I ask.

She nods. "That's it!"

I am quite relieved. *Okay,* I think, *time to face the music.* I gingerly pull down on the bandages to have a look.

It's just like she said it would be. "Wow!" I exclaim. "This isn't so bad after all. You described it perfectly!" This is not the gross, concave crater I feared. It's like the breasts I had when I was twelve, sort of. I will not be deformed. I breathe a sigh of relief.

I realize in this moment how much reality has shifted for me over the past four years: the me I was before having Lauren would have been horrified by what's been done to me; the me I am today is delighted that my mutilation is only partial, not complete. How one's perspective changes based on circumstance.

Prior to my surgery, I met with KB Mann to tell him about my diagnosis.

"Sadly, Liz, I am not surprised," he said. "I did try to give you a warning that something might happen if you became pregnant too soon. With all of the stress that your body has endured these past few years, your immune system is compromised. Adding the burden of pregnancy likely put your body over its tipping point."

"What's done is done," I said. And then I asked him the questions that were really on my mind: "Where do I stand going forward? Will the baby be okay? Will I be able to fight this cancer and have a long life?"

He thought a long time before answering. "Liz," he finally began, "please know that I can't guarantee you anything—but I do see that you are strong and that you will fight. The key thing is to take care of your body for the rest of your life. It is especially important now, just after this surgery, to build up your immune system and to have excellent nutrition. Avoid processed foods that are laden with chemicals, avoid sugars and fats, eat as healthy as possible, and exercise, even if it is just walking every day."

He wrote down instructions for me. "I am going to give you a homeopathic solution to take just before your surgery that will stimulate your body's healing and repair," he said. "It is called *Arnica montana*. After your chemotherapy is complete, I want to see you on a regular basis to put you on an eighteen-month regimen of homeopathic remedies that will purge the residue of the chemotherapy toxins from your body and strengthen your immune system. If you follow this simple advice, I think that both you and your baby will have long and healthy lives."

I left KB's office that day with optimism, and I did take his homeopathic remedy before my surgery, as instructed. Now, weeks later, after taking this remedy and applying vitamin E to my scar daily, my scar has healed remarkably well—all my doctors have commented on how amazing it is.

I remind myself that after I complete chemo and recover my strength, I can have breast reconstruction surgery done, and then, I'm sure, I will look and feel like new. In fact, that gives me something to look forward to, because the procedure that I am considering is one where the plastic surgeon will take my abdominal fat and place it into the mastectomy site. It will be like getting a tummy tuck and a firm new breast at the same time! After the toll of bearing three children, that's a plus. But that is nine to twelve months in the future. For now, I need to prepare for six months of chemotherapy.

The chemo scares me more than anything else, especially after I meet with my oncologist, Dr. Hogan. Because I am pregnant, I will not have radiation, otherwise I'd be Scot's patient. The brochures that describe the toxicity and the side effects of the three-drug chemotherapy cocktail I will be injected with are deeply frightening. I will get an intravenous chemo treatment about one hour in duration every three weeks for six months. I will likely experience nausea, dry or cracked mouth and lips, dry skin, hair loss, fatigue, lack of appetite, risk of excessive bleeding, high risk of sunburn if I go outside, and vision problems.

Although I really have no choice and I trust Scot's research, I can't help but wonder how these toxins might affect my baby. How much of this will enter his system? How might it affect him? The studies that Scot found indicate that some babies exposed to chemo are born small, likely due to the mother's lack of appetite. Some later prove to be a bit slow in their development or learning. But I am willing to take the chance and deal with it when he is born. I am not giving up on my baby now. After an ultrasound, I'm told that he already appears to be a big baby, more than four and a half pounds. Thank God I grow them big!

My first chemo treatment is scheduled for the Thursday before the Fourth of July holiday. My last treatment should be in December, hopefully before Christmas. I like this schedule, because it means that I should be able to start the New Year fresh, without chemo and with a plan for renewed health.

In the spirit of my new resolve to be a fighter and take control, I develop rituals for my chemo treatments and their aftermath, allowing me to cope mentally and physically. I take the chemo late in the day on Thursdays. The effects usually don't kick in for a few hours, so I go home and eat dinner and then lie in bed and watch TV until bedtime. The next day I am in bed all day; I have no strength and am dizzy and fatigued. That is always the worst day, but I know that, so I plan my life accordingly. I have my babysitter come on this day to take care of James, and on the weekends Jim is at home to help me. Each day that passes after the chemo, I regain my strength. I force myself to eat, even when I have absolutely no appetite. I think of the baby that I am carrying and know that he needs nourishment. This gives me the will to eat. I drink water all day to flush out the toxins as quickly as possible.

As each postchemo day passes, I gradually regain my stamina. I set goals of household chores to do or errands to run each day. These are mental and physical exercises that I hope will help keep me strong without overdoing it and endangering my health. By the end of the third week after the treatment, I almost always feel normal. But then, of course, it's time to start the cycle all over again. I accept this as what I need to do for my baby. I have to stay strong, so I do.

As we did the summer after Lauren died, we spend a good amount of our weekend time at Jeff's mountain home. Because the chemo and my pregnancy make heat affect me more now, I appreciate the cool, crisp air. The location also allows us to swim in privacy without me worrying about my appearance. When I am at a pool with friends at home, I have to slip padding into my maternity bathing suit cup, and I worry about it moving around or popping out. It's a comfort to be around friends and family who know us well and who care deeply about us. It is especially nice for Jim and little James to be around their siblings and cousins, too, especially when I go through my fatigue cycles. It's no fun for them to sit around with me when I am not up for much activity.

Throughout the summer, I feel fortunate to have support from so many caring people: friends and family, Maureen (my Living Beyond Breast Cancer mentor), and friends of friends who have been through breast cancer. People at church have put me on the prayer list. Friends from the Down syndrome group and the Arc Alliance send notes and call. It is uplifting to feel so much love and positive energy. This outpouring of support keeps me in a upbeat frame of mind and helps me through this difficult journey.

My hair is falling out—more and more each day. What is left looks dry and dull. Because my hair is so thick, I don't go bald immediately. It just seems to thin every day. As per recommendations from my Living Beyond Breast Cancer mentor, I went to a wig shop before my chemo began to be fitted for a full wig. It's important to go before chemo so the wigmakers can take your photo and a snippet of your hair for color and texture, and help you choose a wig that is most similar to your own hair.

I've chosen a full, shoulder-length wig and had it permed to a style much like my own. I spent the money to buy a good wig of human hair because, quite frankly, losing my hair has been more devastating to me than losing my breast. No one except Jim sees my breast. *Everyone* sees my head. I don't want people to stare at me.

I've decided that a quality wig will do me an enormous amount of psychological good and keep me in a positive frame of mind.

I am lucky enough to get through the hot summer months with a light, partial wig and scarves. But by fall, all of my long hair is gone and I need the full wig. Even as my long hair falls out, though, I am growing back new hair. So I am never completely bald, which I feel fortunate about. I was surprised at how chilly I was in cold weather with little hair! I marveled at how I grossly underestimated the anatomy of my body. I always wear my wig when I go out, but around the house I just wear knit caps to keep my head warm.

Toward the end of September, Dr. Hogan consults with my ob-gyn practice to schedule a delivery date. This is how they do it for mothers who are diabetic or who have other risk factors—like cancer. They don't want me to go into labor in an uncontrolled setting. They have concerns for my health and strength due to side effects of chemotherapy. They don't want me to undergo a long or strenuous labor and the potential for excessive bleeding or trauma. We pick a date two weeks prior to my actual due date.

I will go in for an induced delivery using a gel applied to my cervix to bring on labor. My baby is a very healthy size now and should be seven to eight pounds by that time. If the gel does not bring on labor, I will need to have a cesarean section. I tell my surgeon that if I do have a C-section, I would like my tubes tied while he's in there. My eventual breast reconstruction will mean I won't be able to have another baby via C-section; having my tubes tied will eliminate future worry about an unplanned pregnancy. Much as I would love to have more children, it's just not in the cards.

After delivery and some rest, I will have my final four chemo treatments. By the end of the year, I will be done.

My son's birth day is set for Wednesday, September 26. I am excited to hold my baby, but I am also worried about how the chemotherapy may have affected him. I pray that he has not been physically or (more important) mentally harmed from this trauma.

Throughout all of this, our friends, the Leiths, have been supportive of us. Their daughter, Chris, who is a maternity nurse at the hospital where I will deliver, comes to my house the day before I am admitted to help me complete the necessary paperwork. She has asked to work that day so that she can be with me for my delivery. I am comforted to know a friend will be there.

When we arrive at the hospital on the big morning, Chris greets Jim and me and gives me a big hug. As I settle in on the bed, the doctor comes in with the gel. He explains that it should work within thirty minutes. If not, we'll talk about other options. He inserts the gel and then leaves to attend to another patient. Thankfully, Chris stays by my side, because in just ten minutes, my contractions start. I am in full labor in no time.

Labor progresses quickly, and I am grateful that Chris is with me. For the next hour, she coaches me, and the doctor pops in to check on me from time to time. The birthing process is moving along just fine, and at this point I have no need for pain medication. Then, suddenly, I am at the pushing stage. My doctor gets in a sitting position to deliver our baby. With a few strong pushes, our precious baby boy is out and born!

I've kept my eyes closed during my pushing; I've never really cared to see the messy childbirth process. Before I open my eyes to see the baby, I ask Chris if he is normal and healthy looking. She says he is absolutely beautiful and looks quite healthy, with a full head of hair. "Thank God, thank God, thank God," I say over and over again.

Jim brings me our son. He is indeed a beautiful, healthy-looking baby, chubby and perfect. He weighs in at eight pounds, which is pretty amazing considering the fact that he was born two weeks early. Because my arms are weak, Jim holds him for a while and then puts him down on the bed next to me so we can cuddle. I feel sorry that I can't breast-feed him—I can't even do it with my healthy breast because of my chemo treatments. But he seems perfectly content sleeping next to me.

Please, let him be as healthy as he looks, I pray silently.

Jim leaves to call our parents to share the good news while Chris wheels my bed into my room on the maternity floor.

Because of my hair loss and my mastectomy, I am given a private room. Jim returns and we talk about a name for our son. We are torn between Keith and Bryan. One thing we know: we want to give our son the middle name Scot, after Dr. Scot Fisher. We decide to flip a coin and let fate decide. Fate owes us a few.

The coin toss comes up for "Bryan." It's decided. Our beautiful new baby boy is named Bryan Scot Barker. He weighs eight pounds and one ounce and is twenty-one inches long. He is perfect.

I think of how close we came to missing out on this. Rather than celebrating this day, we could be mourning an aborted pregnancy. Never again will we take any medical professional's advice unquestioningly. We are forever grateful to Scot for the gift of our son. It feels like we have finally emerged from the valley of the shadow into which we descended nearly five years ago.

I now need to get through my last four chemo treatments while juggling a newborn and an active toddler. A daunting scenario for some, but I know that as long as I have my two healthy sons and a loving family surrounding me, I will manage.

Juggling Act

I am joyfully anticipating my homecoming after my brief maternity stay. I'm grateful that the hospital was compassionate enough to not give me a roommate. I've certainly got a lot of issues that I don't feel like rehashing or sharing with even the kindest of new acquaintances. My hair is almost gone, and I need to wear a head covering lest I freak out the maternity ward. I can't breast-feed, and I don't feel like explaining why. Although I am very grateful and relieved that Bryan and I are okay, it is still a bit sad for me to have yet another maternity experience gone awry and for it to not be the stuff of my dreams. Even though the birthing experience with James was "normal," there was a cloud of dread hanging over my head during and after my pregnancy with him because I knew that within two months of his birth, Lauren would go in for a significant heart surgery. This time, with Bryan, I'm dealing with my own health issues. And I won't be able to have another baby now. This is it.

I arrive home to see that my sister-in-law Lynn has thoughtfully decorated the entire front of our house in blue, signaling to our neighbors that we are celebrating the birth of a healthy baby boy. In my sentimental homecoming photo, with Bryan in my arms and toddler James hanging on to my leg, I still look seven months pregnant. It's quite a difference in my postpartum shape from Lauren's birth, when I shed the weight in a snap due to stress. But hey, losing my baby fat is the least of my worries now.

It's the end of September, and my treatment schedule dictates four more rounds of chemo, each one spaced three weeks apart. This means my treatments will end just before Christmas. What a great Christmas present—to be done with chemo! This will be perfect timing. I can start the New Year with a clean slate and hopefully with a clean bill of health, too.

As the treatments have progressed, the chemo has taxed my body more and more, and the demands of motherhood exacerbate it. I develop mouth sores. My eyesight gets blurry when I am tired, and there are times when I literally feel like my eyes are rolling up into my head. This has happened to me once while I was driving— a frightening experience. I am also worried that the side effects of chemo will be worse now that I am not pregnant. One of the women I spoke with in a support group said that her chemo side effects were more intense after she delivered her baby. This plays on my mind because so far I have not experienced the violent nausea that is often associated with chemo, and I'm concerned that I will now. With Bryan growing inside me, I was very conscientious to make sure that I ate well. I dread my first treatment "going solo," without my pregnancy to motivate me.

Somehow I make it through these last weeks of chemo cycles despite juggling a newborn and an active toddler. I keep the same routine for my treatments that I had prior to my delivery. Taking the chemo late Thursday afternoons works well, and I am lucky to have a wonderful part-time babysitter, Jenice, to assist me. She is a mature woman who cares for my sons as if they were her own. I have disability leave from work, again, and that insurance pay, at two thirds of what I'd normally earn, is enough for us, especially since we are not out and about as much these days. And because I am home, I can plan better to prepare home-cooked meals, which saves money and is healthier, too.

We exercise as a family several times per week. We simply load up the boys in their double stroller and head to our nearby Wissahickon Valley Park after Jim arrives home from work on weekdays or in the morning on weekends. If I am in my later part of the treatment cycle and have energy, we walk about two miles. In the earlier days of my cycles, I either don't go along with the boys, or I walk a bit and then they go ahead without me while I sit and enjoy the park solo. Regardless of what I am capable of on any given day, being in that park is therapeutic. I am happy there—appreciative of the sights, sounds, and smells of nature around me. It reminds me of how grateful I am that both Bryan and I are alive and well. Spending time at the Wissahickon gives a sense of focus and peace I don't find anywhere else during these chaotic days.

Each time, as soon as we stop the car at the park, little James is anxious to be freed from his car seat and raring to get out and run. He usually runs the whole trail length going out but then rides back in the stroller with baby Bryan when he's spent. We all love the Wissahickon. Although it is not a playground and has no amenities, it is nature's playground. Its wide walking trail is bordered on one side by the Wissahickon creek and on the other by steep inclines and rugged trails that we can't navigate with our stroller. One day, I think, when the boys are older and I am healthy, we can hike those trails together. Maybe the boys will wade in the creek, too, as I did when I was younger. And hopefully I will be able to look back on this time now with fond memories of the park as a healing and reenergizing place.

Between eating healthy, exercising, and being as active as I can to keep up with caring for my sons, the pregnancy weight melts off. I remind myself to keep fit because I will be facing major surgery in the spring when I go in for my reconstruction. I was advised to give my body some recovery time after the chemo treatments ended to build up my strength and my immune system.

Although I am faring well with it, the chemo is silently taking its toll. I notice this at Christmastime when I am nearing my last treatment. With the usual extra stress associated with the holiday—shopping, decorating, cooking, etc.—I am feeling the side effects much more than I have in the past months. From the combination of dry, heated air inside and all the socializing and talking I'm doing, my mouth sores have become a greater nuisance. But as always, I remain optimistic and dwell on the positive: the fact that my last treatment will be a week prior to Christmas. This means that I'll be on the rebound by Christmas. My final treatment is scheduled for the day after we have James's birthday party. So I'll be at my most energetic for having the families over for this gathering. These little blessings keep me going.

We enjoy a wonderful Christmas as a little family: James is an excited toddler, and three-month-old Bryan is taking it all in with his big eyes. It's like a rerun of another Christmas when we had Lauren as a toddler and James as the wide-eyed baby. I miss Lauren not being with us, but I am—thankfully—not as sad as I was last year at this time. Instead, I'm feeling grateful that I have made it through this year's ordeal and that Bryan is healthy. After all the drama and turmoil, our greatest gifts are being together and happy. Material things are meaningless to us right now. Our Christmas wish list has just one item on it: for me to recover well and remain cancer-free for many years ahead. More than anything else, we desperately want our sons to grow up with two loving parents.

Naturally, at these special holiday times, thoughts and memories of Lauren come back. I think how happy she'd be if she were here with us, being the big sister to her two brothers. How she loved her special Christmas dress and shoes, and her cozy Christmas pajamas, too. As I pulled out my Christmas decorations this year, the floodgates of emotions opened, and I tearfully caressed the little holiday things that she made in her preschool—her photo ornaments, her Christmas stocking—and vowed to faithfully put these out and on my tree each year, even when I am an old lady. I made a commitment to continue my tradition of special ornaments for and about the boys, as the years ahead unfold, to be displayed alongside Lauren's special things.

All in all, it is a good Christmas. I look forward to the New Year, to being done with the chemo and with my recovery from it. *Maybe in this New Year our luck will change and we will finally break free of this vicious cycle of misfortune,* I think, ever hopeful.

After Christmas, as I put away our decorations, I decide to start an annual tradition for this postholiday packing-up time. Each year, I will take the time to reflect on the prior year's events—all of them, good, bad, or indifferent—and be thankful for my life and the fact that I have the health to enjoy it. Then I'll contemplate the coming year.

This year, as I carefully wrap Lauren's ornaments in tissue paper and place them in a box, I wonder: What will the upcoming New Year be like? Will I remain well and in remission? How will the boys, especially Bryan, grow and change? I know the looking-ahead part will be difficult. How can I ever not fear the cancer coming back? Worse yet, will my past chemo treatments affect Bryan down the line? Although I know I must remain optimistic to encourage mind and body healing, it is impossible to not worry. My New Year's resolution is to think positive.

My usual superwoman stamina left me months ago when treatment started. The fatigue I feel—from the chemo, but also from pregnancy, surgery, and a life as a busy mom—is intense. By each day's end, I am completely wiped out. But I accept my exhaustion willingly, knowing that I have my life back.

The quiet winter season is a perfect time for me to be home and to heal mentally and physically. The toxic chemo treatments are done, my hair is regrowing, and I am taking it all in stride to build up stamina for my reconstruction surgery in the spring. My postchemo oncology visits have gone just fine: both Bryan and I are thriving, me with my hair returning and he developing just as he should for his age. He is a chubby and very happy baby. While I am still concerned about how his being exposed to the chemo while in utero might have affected him, there are no signs of any developmental delays so far. What haunts me daily, though, are the doctors' dire predictions that he might be "slow or small." I keep a constant watchful eye on him.

My reconstruction surgery is scheduled for after Easter and just before Lauren's birthday. Because I am always emotional around her birthday, I self-strategize to be in a positive frame of mind going into this major surgery. To help me with this, I make an appointment to consult with KB. I need his reassurance, and I want him to give me another homeopathic remedy to help with my physical healing, like he did for my mastectomy.

With the fearful thoughts of Lauren's postoperative death due to a hospital-acquired infection on my mind, I interview a couple of plastic surgeons for my reconstruction. I choose an earnest, youthful surgeon who spends time with me explaining my options. The reconstruction surgery is a complex procedure. Currently, silicone implants are banned due to malfunctions and health risks—and the truth is, the idea of silicone implants makes me queasy. I opt for the TRAM flap procedure, where my own abdominal fat, muscle, and veins will be rerouted and transplanted to my chest to reconstruct a replacement breast. Later, dark tissue harvested from my inner thigh will be transformed into a nipple.

Fortunately, I have a mentor to guide me—my dear friend Patty, who underwent this same reconstruction surgery this year. She had a different surgeon, but she is about my age, and her experience is fresh in her mind. We get together at her home for lunch and a play-date with our children so she can school me on what I will be facing.

Patty tells me exactly what to expect from presurgery to post-op. She explains the night-before prep of emptying my stomach and intestines with heavy laxatives. How the doctor will come in just before surgery, have me stand up naked in front of him (so that he can see my body alignment as it is), and then use a surgical marking pen to mark incision areas. She explains that post-op will not be pretty. The stitches are ugly. I will be puffy, swollen, and red from collar to pubic area. And somewhat scarier, that I may be stooped and bent over slightly, like an old woman, due to the abdominal-to-chest surgical incisions. And finally, that I will have odd-looking bulbous drains hanging out of my body at the key incision sites. It sounds a bit ghastly but the end result will be worth it, she assures me. She then shows me her breasts after reconstruction, and they do look wonderful. I agree that this surgery will make me feel whole again and restore my self-esteem for hopefully my long life ahead.

Yep, Patty looks toned and youthful, and her hair has grown back beautifully. I leave her house feeling confident and optimistic. I just wish that I look as great as she does post-operatively!

I begin to shake as I am wheeled into the chilly, sterile operating room—not only from the cold but from my fright. I fear infection complications like Lauren had even more than death on the table. The horrid memories of her slow and painful demise still terrify me. I close my eyes and pray to her, my angel, that this complicated surgery will go well.

Thankfully, it does. It goes flawlessly, in fact. The swelling, pain, and not being able to stand up straight are upsetting, but Patty forewarned me of this, so although it's disturbing, I am prepared for it. I'm diligent with my physical therapy and my positive expectations, and my healing progresses as expected. It takes a few weeks for the swelling to subside, but when my body normalizes, I am very satisfied with my results. When summer begins, I am pretty much recovered and ready for the pool and beach.

As an added bonus, I get to do something that I haven't done in years. With this tummy tuck and breast shape-up, I am able to wear a bikini! I am amazed that at age thirty-five, and after bearing three children, I can carry it off. My stomach looks flat and toned, and my new breast perfectly matches the other. But behind that bathing suit, of course, "scar city" is etched all over my body. My newly sculpted breast is encircled with a big elliptical scar, and I have a giant "smile scar" across my abdomen from hip to hip.

My hair, which was previously straight, is coming in soft and wavy like a newborn's. I like this new and natural look. I decide that I will wear my hair short for a while; it's just easier to manage as a busy mom. Between eating healthfully, exercising (really just walking in the park to keep up with James's running), and keeping a positive and happy attitude—which is easy to do, since I find so much joy in the simplicity of being a mom to two healthy sons—I feel the most fit and alive as I have been in years.

Going back to work is inevitable. It's not just about the need for the extra income; it's about retaining the quality health-care plan my employer sponsors. Between Lauren's care and mine, we have seen firsthand how easy it is to rack up a million-dollar tab for a catastrophic illness. Without health insurance, we would be in financial ruin by now.

I also want to keep myself mentally engaged, of course—to move on and beyond our tragic past, and to do work that I enjoy. Worrier that I am, I have concerns about how I will manage my time and remain emotionally and physically fit once I'm working again, but I resolve to figure it out as I go. After taking the summer off to rejuvenate, I return to my job in September. I do so with a flexible schedule that keeps me at the thirty hours needed to maintain my full employee benefits.

I return to work with mixed emotions. I once again feel compelled to explain my absence to coworkers, clients, and other people I do business with, and I dread their reactions. But I am amazed by how kind and caring people are in response to my story. They tell me how well I look. They repeatedly say what a remarkable person I am to have been able to not only survive, but thrive, throughout so much hardship. These conversations jog my memory, and I am reminded of the encouraging talk I had with KB after Lauren's death.

He told me that I would one day be in the public eye, speaking and sharing my story, inspiring others, I remember. *Is it my destiny to turn my story of triumph over tragedy into a book to help others?*

Penning a book will serve many purposes, I decide. It will offer me closure for what I hope to be the last of my life's great challenges. It will allow others, even those who are close to us, to understand the magnitude of the emotional roller coaster that we've been on these five difficult years. How much we needed and appreciated their love, support, and care during the tough times. How their care has sustained us. And documenting my experiences may help others who are experiencing life-altering changes by offering them a message of hope.

I have learned so much after surviving so many hardships: to be tenacious and optimistic in the face of adversity; to trust and follow your natural instincts; to welcome angel moments when they appear; to know that however enormous the hardship at hand, there will be an end to it; and that whatever happens will be a direct result of how you handle the circumstances. As the saying goes, "Life is 10 percent what you make it and 90 percent how you take it."

So I begin to pursue my book quest journey. I research the process to find a literary agent and a publisher. I carefully outline the book, segregated by events and key scenes within the timelines. I eagerly write the first chapter. After several edits, I am quite pleased with my writing and storytelling skills. But my query process—not surprisingly, since I am a first-time, unknown author—produces nothing but rejection letters.

I continuously analyze KB's prediction about my future. He has refused to give me details or a time frame about his prophecy regarding my speaking and storytelling. I begin to suspect that the prominence he predicted is not in my immediate future. After months of effort, I reluctantly file away my writing and work. I don't want to play the role of starving artist. I need to get back to the career that pays the bills and provides us with our lifeline of health insurance. *I'll try again later, when the timing seems right,* I promise myself. I am committed to exploring KB's foretelling. I want to write to honor Lauren's memory and to share the amazing lessons that she taught me in just three short years. But it will have to wait for now.

Little do I know that it will take nearly twenty years before the stars aligned and the timing is right for my book journey to resume.

Going back to work this time, it feels different. It feels permanent. I intuitively sense that all of the bad stuff is behind me now. My gut tells me that my battles are over and it is time for normalcy. Bryan and I have battled fate, faced down death, and won. I am determined to champion our victory and to celebrate the gifts of our lives. Although I was not able to save my daughter from death, I will honor her memory forever, in whatever way I can. One day the book I've written will be the ultimate tribute to her, but for now, I will find daily inspiration in celebrating the victories we have won and will give thanks for what we have each and every day. Everything has happened for a reason. One day, I know, the logic of it all will reveal itself.

From Then to Now

Two to Five Years Out

The first five years after Bryan's birth are happy but busy. I work at rebuilding my career, caring for the boys and our home, and keeping an eye on Bryan's health and mine. Mercifully, at each of their checkups, Bryan and James are revealed to be in perfect physical condition. My semiannual oncology checkups are all fine as well. Per KB's advice, I make the time to exercise as an outlet for stress. I incorporate his regimen of homeopathic care. For eighteen months following my reconstruction surgery, I undertake homeopathic remedies to cleanse out the chemotherapy toxins and to strengthen my immune system. As a result, I feel healthy and fit. By the time I turn forty, I have my old stamina level back. My reconstruction scars fade gradually as well. My first five years in remission warrant annual bone scans and mammograms, which thankfully are always normal.

The pain of losing Lauren eases a bit each year, but I can't imagine ever forgetting our time together. I simply accept that I can't be sad anymore, or live in the past. I will always remember her, but with happy, loving thoughts, not regret. My boys need me now. I need to keep a positive attitude to maintain my health.

I manage to keep in touch with my Arc friends, and I continue to volunteer and support their annual fund-raising events. In a heartwarming gesture, many of our family members send a donation to the Arc Alliance in Lauren's memory at each Christmas and on her birthday. I enroll in a payroll deduction program with the United Way and designate the Arc as my recipient.

I attend the semiannual Living Beyond Breast Cancer conferences to learn more about breast cancer and its aftermath. I am a bit afraid of getting too involved there. Not only do I have limited time juggling work and home life, I am fearful that I will meet women who are not doing well with treatment or who may be dying. I feel guilty about this, especially since LBBC was supportive of me when I was going through treatment. But until I hit the magic five-year mark in remission, I can't help being a bit apprehensive about my own health, and I'm not sure I can handle befriending women whose health is declining.

Because I was pregnant while diagnosed, it is hard to discern if my cancer was estrogen driven or not. My lack of a family history of cancer and my diagnosis at such a young age creates many unanswered questions. That's why it is important to share what my personality is like. I believe that it *is* a reason that I stress out, and this could have invited cancer in. But, ultimately, I am convinced that my cancer was brought on by extraordinary stress: Lauren's unexpected birth defects and death; my ectopic pregnancy and ensuing hepatitis B diagnosis; three pregnancies in five years; and the massive pressures of dealing with my HMO, reluctant doctors, and endless uncertainty. I suspect that these events formed the perfect storm and allowed cancer to attack my weakened immune system. I am now adamant that maintaining a positive mental outlook is the key to my keeping well. Running after my boys will surely see to that!

Five to Ten Years Out

Although my company has been a stellar support to me throughout my crises, I have been with them for fifteen years now, and I feel it is time to move on. There have been corporate and management changes during my multiple absences, and besides, I lost a great deal of momentum with all of my downtime. I crave a fresh start. When

Bryan enters a full-day kindergarten program, I make my move. The parting is amicable.

I become a financial advisor with the top bank in our region, and it is a welcome new challenge. But my compensation is commission driven, which has both good and bad points: on the one hand, I can make my own schedule and have time for the boys and their activities; on the other hand, there is no salary, just commissions, renewals, and the constant need for new business.

I still yearn to have a daughter. Both my boys are so sweet and good, but I miss the bond I shared with Lauren. The short time that we had together as mother and daughter was different from the time I've had with Bryan and James. I ask my oncologist, who is about my age and a mother of three sons herself, about pregnancy postcancer and postsurgery.

She remains composed and professional, but clearly thinks it is a daring question. "Aren't you worried about what might happen?" she asks.

"Of course," I say. "I just want a daughter so badly."

"Well, statistically speaking, pregnancy after all you've been through is rare," she states.

"What would you do?" I ask.

"Actually," she confides, "I'm in the process of adopting two young sisters from Russia. I want daughters, too." She smiles.

Hmm, I think. *Adoption would be a great solution.* I begin to explore the idea of adopting a baby girl from Korea through Pearl S. Buck International. But just as I begin to get more serious about it, my work demands suddenly increase dramatically. Overwhelmed, I let this dream go. It is a decision I will eventually regret.

In the year that Lauren would have been ten years old, Debby and I chair the Arc Alliance parents' group annual dinner dance and to dedicate it to Lauren's memory. On the home front, we decide that James and Bryan should have their own rooms, so we convert the former nursery into Bryan's room. We break down the bunk beds from James's room, buy Bryan some additional furniture, and lovingly pack away Lauren's clothes, along with some of my favorite baby clothing from all three children that I want as keepsakes. The dolls and girl toys that neither of the boys will want as they grow older I pack up or bag for donation. It is another fresh start.

Regardless of my busy schedule, year in and year out I am conscientious about my follow-up appointments with my oncologist. I see her twice a year for checkups, blood tests, and a mammogram. Fortunately, I am well. So are the boys. They are both developing exactly as they should physically and mentally. Looking back now, it is bizarre, and a bit surreal, that we had such a horrible run of bad luck for those five consecutive years. Replaying those past scenarios is frightening. Why did so much go wrong in succession as it did? How did we manage to survive it? We have all recovered and thrived these past ten years, but I know how quickly that can change. I pray that our lives remain on this even keel and that our stormy years are over for good.

Ten to Fifteen Years Out

As the boys progress from grade school to high school, I am consistently an active parent and volunteer. I relish all of it: the fall festivities with pumpkin patches and Halloween parties; the holiday festivals with food and events; talent shows; art and music events; sports; field trips; book fairs. Regardless of the role—classroom aide, spaghetti dinner server, bingo chairperson, or yard monitor—I do it all while juggling my home and career responsibilities. Perhaps my past tragedy puts this busy life into perspective. I don't know what my future holds, or how long I will be in remission, so I want to take in as much of life as I can each day. I appreciate and take pleasure in the simple joys of my children's lives. Most times, I am exhausted at day's end. But keeping busy in this way leaves me no time to dwell on the past or mourn my losses. It keeps me upbeat and moving forward daily.

In high school, the boys become rowers, in keeping with the

Barker family legacy. Both their dad and their grandfather, James
J. Barker Sr., were championship oarsmen in their day, and James
and Bryan turn out to be talented oarsmen as well. They each win
a prestigious Stotesbury Regatta championship medal. Naturally, I
am involved with their teams and a constant volunteer at these crew
regattas. Jim and his dad, meanwhile, are the coaches at Bryan's
school, the Haverford School. They call me "the cupcake lady"
because I always bake the frosted treats for school events.

The boys' high school years pass in a whirlwind of activity—
dances, sporting events, dating, driving, proms, college tours,
graduation, and senior week.

How did these years fly by so quickly? I silently ask myself as I sit
at their graduations. I often stop and reflect on what our lives would
be like if Lauren were still alive, or if we had we proceeded with
adoption. We'd still have a youngster in grade school. Although I
regret my decision to pass on adoption, it is nice to be independent
of babysitters and driving duties as the years progress.

Fifteen to Twenty Years Out

The boys are going on to college. Fortunately, each is admitted to
their first choices: James to Marist College in Poughkeepsie, New
York, and Bryan to the University of Pennsylvania. Both are on their
school's crew teams. I can't help but be amused by what my doctors
initially told me about Bryan eighteen years ago: *"He might be small,
he might be slow."* Not so much. Bryan is a varsity athlete as well
as an honors student who has been admitted to a competitive Ivy
League school.

With all these blessings, not a day goes by that I am not thankful
for Dr. Scot Fisher, who saved both of our lives! I can't imagine what
my mental—and, subsequently, physical—state would be now if I
had followed that initial doctor's advice and not carried Bryan to
term. I shudder to think of it.

Our lives continue to be relatively uneventful. Overall we are
pretty hale and hearty. No chronic problems. Jim and I still question

the strangeness of that horrible spell of health disasters for those long and hard five years. We are grateful for the good fortune we've had since then, however. And I take nothing for granted. I keep all of us on track with our medical, dental, and eye exams. I'm not taking any risks.

Twenty Years Out to Present

Life has been good. Not easy, mind you—just good. No major health issues other than some minor knee surgery for a torn meniscus. I am going through menopause now. Although my symptoms are mild and don't really affect the quality of my life (other than an occasional hot flash, especially after drinking my morning coffee), the change does seem to render me feeling sluggish. In photos of myself, I think that my face looks "full." My fitted work wardrobe pieces are starting to feel tight and annoying. This affects my outlook and well-being.

I still remember KB's warning—*"The key thing is to take care of your body for the rest of your life"*—and it moves me to take action. There is a yoga studio down the road from my office. *Perfect location,* I think. It's literally on my way home, so there will be no avoiding it. I sign up for their month-long New to Yoga series and I fall in love with yoga practice. It is wonderful to go to the studio after a stressful workday. Not only is yoga a nice body workout, it also clears the mind of stress. And the more I do it, the better I look and feel. My face thins. My clothes fit better now, and some even have a loose waistline. People are commenting that I look different. It's a wonderful feeling.

Practicing yoga invigorates me so much, physically and mentally, that I come up with an ambitious plan. The year 2011 will mark what would have been Lauren's twenty-fifth birthday. I am yearning to do something to commemorate her life and her memory. I call the Arc Alliance and ask if I can chair a committee to host a fund-raising dinner dance, as we had done in the past. Paul Stengle, who was the director when Lauren was alive and is still there, just as dedicated as ever, enthusiastically endorses my plan and offers the help of his staff to form our event committee. Planning the dinner dance is certainly a great deal of work, but it is a joy. I am thrilled to have this opportunity to bring together a crowd of good friends, family, and those who knew and loved Lauren to celebrate what would have been a landmark birthday. It truly warms my heart to celebrate and share her special life that touched so many of us. I make a giant collage of her best photos to display that evening and compose a loving tribute to her in the program book. On the night of the event, I reminisce fondly about my daughter before the crowd. A few tears are shed, but it's all good, I am among friends.

We receive tremendous positive feedback from all of the attendees. Many of them say that this has been one of the best parties that they have attended in a long while. I am literally glowing with euphoria! The positive energy I'm feeling is downright magical. Between this success and the exhilaration inspired by my yoga practice, I experience a life-altering revelation. I am suddenly inspired to dust off my longtime dream—I need to write my book! Could it be that my stars are aligned now? Is this finally the right time to fulfill KB's prophecy? I can't ask him about this, or for his advice. Many years ago, he moved back to his native India, and I lost track of him. But I decide to trust my instincts. *This is it,* I think. *It's time.*

My dream never went away. It just faded a bit while I was busy rebuilding my strength and my life. I did the initial work years ago—outlined the book, wrote the first chapter, and so on. I just need to dust it off and pick up where I left off. My book quest has always been with me, waiting for its chance. And now the experiences I've had in the past few months have lit my fire. How cosmic it is that my act of charity—giving back to the Arc in honor of Lauren's birthday—has, in turn, given back to me this gift of renewed energy and drive to follow my dream! My yoga teachers often instruct us to put our wishes out there into the universe and let the law of attraction happen. I believe that this is what has occurred here.

In his cryptic predictions, KB stated that I would become a successful public spokesperson, sharing my information and knowledge. As a result of this, he said, I would have the opportunity to be philanthropic and to promote charitable organizations. "Good things will come to you in due time, Liz. Be patient," he said. "These things will occur at a ripe time in your life when you are most able to appreciate them."

For twenty-plus years, I've patiently waited for this time to come. With my radar on, searching for clues and any opportunity to seize, I have anticipated the moment that my book journey would resume. Could this be another perfect storm forming—but this time, a positive one? Is this Lauren thanking me? Was this event meant to teach and inspire me to follow my dream and to fulfill KB's prediction? Is it possible that my altruistic fund-raiser is now paying it forward to me? Only time will tell. Because you are reading this book, it is evident that I have completed the book quest part of my life journey. But there will be more to come. I hope that you will continue on this journey with me.

Namaste

Acknowledgments

This story isn't necessarily just about me or my challenges or accomplishments. It's about the journey and the life lessons one learns when becoming a champion. It's about how each one of you has supported me along this long and difficult path with your love, kindness, and care. I want to express heartfelt thanks to all of you!

I'll start my chain of gratitude from the beginning, with my family.

To my parents, who sacrificed to provide for us and who instilled good values in our moral compasses. To my four siblings, especially Rosemarie, thank you for your ongoing love and loyalty. To my dear husband, Jim, thank you for your unwavering dedication to and love for me. For my sons, James and Bryan, you are the lights of my life. For all of my in-laws, your love and acceptance of me into your family is indisputable. You have been rocks for Jim and me over the years.

To our many good friends who have remained so throughout the years as we have all navigated through our busy lives, thank you for your steadfastness. In particular, I want to recognize my gal pals from Mount St. Joseph Academy and Jim's buddies from St. Joseph's Prep, our respective high schools. I also want to mention our wonderful neighbors from the Thornhill Drive/Briar Lane group. I offer particular appreciation to Jeff Barker and Deborah Moorehead Irons (Lauren's godparents); Dan and Ginny Mulhern; Carol Sztukowski Ponzek; Tom and Denise Toland; and all of our Roxborough group members from back in the day.

Perhaps I was distracted, tired, upset, or anxious at times over the years, but after reading this book, I think that you may better understand why. Forgive me if I wasn't always on or there for you. Please know that your care and companionship gave us the strength to cope.

I have nothing but gratitude for my employer, AXA Equitable, during the difficult years I've described in this book. Without their fine health and disability benefits and accommodation of my absences, Jim and I would have been ruined financially. I especially want to recognize my Equitable mentors, the late Hank Gartner and Bernie Encarnacion Sr., who gave me my initial chance and a helping hand to success. I also want to remember the late Bridget Ferraioli, who was an outstanding assistant and a good friend for years before she succumbed to breast cancer.

After Lauren's birth, new friends welcomed us into the world of special needs, especially our mentors Dave and Pat Patterson. We would have been lost and despondent without all of the wonderful acquaintances and staff from the Arc Alliance, KenCrest, the Down Syndrome Interest Group, and Special Olympics. Special needs teachers and therapists are truly special themselves. Thank you for your extraordinary skills and patience and for always being there for us and our children. Warm regards to the Arc's Connie Viens, Kate Kurtz, Charleen McGrath, Scott Camilleri, and Paul Stengle, who were instrumental in the success of the 2011 Fun(d)raiser in Lauren's memory that inspired me to move forward with my book quest.

Later on in my life's journey, when I was diagnosed with breast cancer, I again needed help in finding my way in a new world. This time it was LBBC, Living Beyond Breast Cancer, that offered Jim and me support and guidance. This nonprofit organization is a godsend to those newly diagnosed as well as to longtime survivors like me. Thank you Marissa Weiss for founding it. I also want to thank Patty English for being a mentor throughout my treatment.

There are two very special people in this story who literally swooped in to save both Bryan's and my life. One was a complete stranger I have called Robin out of respect for her privacy. The other was a longtime family friend, Scot Fisher, DO. As the book will explain, Robin saved my life, while Scot saved Bryan's life. I sincerely hope that you both understand the magnitude of your acts of kindness and how you have changed history, and my life in particular, through those acts.

My original idea and inspiration for this book happened shortly after Lauren died. It came from astrologer KB Mann, who is now in India. It was he who gave me a prophecy for this eventual book quest. He guided me to homeopathic care and gave me sage advice that has helped me become a twenty-plus-years survivor. I hope that he is alive and well to read this. We lost touch when he moved back to India many years ago.

Additionally, I'd like to recognize several professional women who have been mentors and instrumental in encouraging me to restart my book quest this past year. They are author and speaker Barbara Greenspan Shaiman; past PWR President Melissa Dietrich; Forum of Executive Women members Linda Stone, Renee Chesler, and the late Judy Grossman; two social media experts who have helped mastermind my blog and branding, Shannon Myers and Kristin Kane Ford; Gina Bacci for her proofreading and encouragement; and speaker and author promoter Nancy P. Ottaviano, who introduced me to my writing collaborator.

My most important thanks go to Tim Vandehey, professional writer and "book doctor," who collaborated with me on this project. Tim, thank you for taking a chance with me and for making this book a champion. Your skills and expertise, coupled with your enduring patience, are very much appreciated. Your professional guidance has allowed me to realize my long-term dream of writing this book and doing it well.

Lastly, I want to thank several people who helped me create my image and branding: the talented graphic artist Lindsay Strippoli of Torn Leaf Designs, LLC for my cover rendition; expert stylist Gus Marrone of John Augustine salon; phenomenal photographer Joanne Posse; makeup artist Robert Francis from La Bella Vita Salon; videographer Ed Seiders of Branded Productions, for creating my video; and again, Shannon Myers and Kristin Kane Ford for my overall branding strategies. These 2 women have been my steadfast angels throughout this long and arduous book quest journey. There were many times when I would not have been able to go on, if it were not for them. Thank you Brooke Warner, publisher of She Writes Press, for taking me and other aspiring women authors under your wing and guiding us to publish our dreams. All of your staff—Cait Levin, Crystal Patriache, Krissa Lagos, have been wonderful.

About the Author

© Joanne Posse photography

Elizabeth Barker is a Philadelphia native and a lifelong resident of the City of Brotherly Love. She has worked for more than twenty-five years as a financial advisor gathering assets as well as accolades for her efforts. Liz has risen in the ranks and has earned the title of vice president at her present firm. Publicly, for five consecutive years, she has been chosen as a Five Star Wealth Manager by Five Star Professional and *Philadelphia* magazine. Liz is active in numerous professional, business, and community organizations, including Professional Women's Roundtable, Whitemarsh Business Association, Living Beyond Breast Cancer, Women Owned Business Network, Women on Course, Network Now, FemFessionals, MSJA Alumnae, Forum of Executive Women, WIBSN, and the ARC Alliance.

What is most remarkable about Liz's accomplishments is that she was able to achieve all of the above while juggling roles as a new mother with a special needs child and as a wife battling breast cancer. Her extraordinary and often mystical encounters with fate inspired her to recount her dramatic life story in her first memoir. She is eager to share her life lessons learned for the benefit of others.

A consummate professional, Liz has performed numerous speaking engagements in her career and has been a guest on radio and TV shows regarding her story. You can find her on her blog at www.changedbychance.com and on Twitter: @lizbychoice.

SELECTED TITLES FROM SHE WRITES PRESS

She Writes Press is an independent publishing company
founded to serve women writers everywhere.
Visit us at www.shewritespress.com.

Breathe: A Memoir of Motherhood, Death, and Family Conflict by Kelly Kittel
$16.95, 978-1-938314-78-0
A mother's heartbreaking account of losing two sons in the span of
nine months—and learning, despite all the obstacles in her way, to find
joy in life again.

A Leg to Stand On: An Amputee's Walk into Motherhood by Colleen Haggerty
$16.95, 978-1-63152-923-8
Haggerty's candid story of how she overcame the pain of losing a leg at
seventeen—and of terminating two pregnancies as a young woman—
and went on to become a mother, despite her fears.

Fire Season: A Memoir by Hollye Dexter
$16.95, 978-1-63152-974-0
After she loses everything in a fire, Hollye Dexter's life spirals down-
ward and she begins to unravel—but when she finds herself at the brink
of losing her husband, she is forced to dig within herself for the strength
to keep her family together.

Seeing Red: A Woman's Quest for Truth, Power, and the Sacred by Lone Morch
$16.95, 978-1-938314-12-4
One woman's journey over inner and outer mountains—a quest that
takes her to the holy Mt. Kailas in Tibet, through a seven-year marriage, and into the arms of the fierce goddess Kali, where she discovers
her powerful, feminine self.

Splitting the Difference: A Heart-Shaped Memoir by Tré Miller-Rodríguez
$19.95, 978-1-938314-20-9
When 34-year-old Tré Miller-Rodríguez's husband dies suddenly from
a heart attack, her grief sends her on an unexpected journey that cul-
minates in a reunion with the biological daughter she gave up at 18.

Think Better. Live Better. 5 Steps to Your Best Life by Francine Huss
$16.95, 978-1-938314-66-7
With the help of this guide, readers will learn to cultivate more creative
thoughts, realign their mindset, and gain a new perspective on life.